HOW TO SUCCEED
WHERE STRONG MEN FAIL

How To
SUCCEED
WHERE
STRONG
MEN FAIL

AVOIDING THE SAMSON TRAP

MARK JOHNSON

Harold Shaw Publishers
Wheaton, Illinois

ISBN 0-87788-742-X

Edited by Robert Bittner

Cover design by David LaPlaca

Library of Congress Cataloging-in-Publication Data

Johnson, Mark, 1947-
    How to succeed where strong men fail : avoiding the Samson trap / Mark Johnson
        p.   cm.
    Includes bibliographical references.
    1. Men—religious life. 2. Samson (Biblical judge) 3. Masculinity—Religious
aspects—Christianity. I. Title.
    BV4528.2.J65 1997
    248.8'42—DC21   97-17004
                                                                        CIP

---

03   02   01   00   99   98   97

10   9   8   7   6   5   4   3   2   1

CONTENTS

PREFACE

This book has been written out of my belief that the tenets of faith in Jesus Christ and the gifts of his Holy Spirit, as highlighted throughout the Bible, represent God's solution for the problems we men face today. We can only come to a place of rest in our souls as we grow in faith and begin to truly comprehend that God is able to "supply all [our] need according to his riches in glory by Christ Jesus" (Phil. 4:19).

These spiritual riches include the promised Holy Spirit whose aim is to transform us into the likeness of Christ. We see in Scripture that the Holy Spirit generally helps us grow in faith through the application of the Christian disciplines in our life such as prayer, fasting, fellowship, Bible study, and the "gifts of the Spirit."

Spiritual gifts are ways the Holy Spirit may choose to manifest himself and demonstrate his presence and power in a person's life. In this regard, I believe that the gift of speaking in tongues (as a manifestation) is extremely relevant for Christians today, as I discuss more fully in chapter 13. Though not for everyone, I have found that the gift of tongues is one of the means God has of translating us out of our ordinary way of viewing things and into an extraordinary appreciation of how the Lord is able to do more for us than we could ever ask or even imagine (Eph. 3:10). To him be the glory.

INTRODUCTION: WHAT IS THE SAMSON TRAP?

This book attempts to explore a painful condition that burdens all men. I have labeled it the *Samson Trap*. In brief, this condition has to do with how afraid we men are and how desperately we seek to hide from our fear. Fear is a core issue for men simply because we are members of the human race; fear constitutes one of our basic emotions. But, thanks to our gene pool, fear also represents a major obstacle to our spiritual and emotional growth.

Being men means the raw nerve of fear isn't something we readily talk about—it seems unmanly. Women can be afraid and start a self-help group. We, on the other hand, are stuck with thinking that we'll just have to bluff our way through those situations that scare us the most. And what scares us more often than not is having to explore any hint of vulnerability.

Hiding from fear certainly characterizes the inmates I work with. I am a psychologist on the correctional mental health team of the Central Jail of Orange County, California. Here, I have daily exposure to over 5,000 inmates whose lives serve as a testimonial to the danger of not facing one's issues constructively. This is particularly the case with fear. As long as trepidation remains an emotional handicap that goes untreated, we men will not be able to achieve the joy, success, or fulfillment we seek in order to feel whole.

In jail and out, I have heard accounts of how fear can grip us early in life due to violence in our homes or in our streets and neighborhoods. Such fear may cause us to become equally violent. Other fears may compel us to seek solace in drugs when we discover that school is no solution for feelings of inadequacy we can't escape; rather, failure in the classroom only compounds the awful feelings inside. Certainly fears over not knowing how to connect with other human beings force us into becoming loners. Hurt and anger over thinking that nobody really cares spawns the need to rebel and get even.

Whatever our "rap sheets" indicate, fears of all kinds can be easily covered up by bravado. Wayward lifestyles help the average male deny his pain, loneliness, anger, and any hunger of the soul that might surface. This seems to be the case for the convicts I encounter. Their life of crime is just an extension of their decision to keep the truth of their frailty a secret. Once behind bars, inmates have to act tough just to survive. But this survival tactic is not something that only characterizes convicts. It is also the means of survival for the majority of men I know or have had the opportunity to see as a clinician during the past twenty-five years. Ironically, these men who live life on the outside are no more free than the men I encounter on the inside. Each group is imprisoned because of fear.

WHERE FEAR BEGAN

I think it is safe to say that every man who has walked this earth has struggled with fears over being seen as inadequate at some level. Such feelings haunt us for good reason. We are spiritually broken; we don't work according to the Manufacturer's specifications.

Our brokenness began in the Garden of Eden, where our earliest ancestors—Adam and Eve—decided to sample the fruit God told them was forbidden. In that moment, his Spirit departed their presence and a void was created in their beings. That void defined who they would be forever. They were indelibly stained by sin and devoid of hope. You see, people were designed to function with God's holy presence as the spiritual glue for keeping their souls intact. Subsequent to the Fall, the human soul was deprived of that glue, and it ultimately turned toward depravity because of humanity's attempts to make do without God.

It didn't work. People remain empty of the very thing their souls hunger for: communion with God. Apart from regaining the fellowship of the Holy Spirit, we are left to try to fill the vacuum inside through pretense and bluster. Not unlike the three-year-old who is convinced he can cross the street by himself, we bank on self-will and pure determination to get us by. Destruction awaits us, but that doesn't matter as long as we get to be in charge of our lives. Meanwhile, fear lurks in the shadows ready to remind us we aren't making it. But that doesn't matter either because fear can be so easily denied. Sadly, we charge ahead to cross that busy intersection, not seeing the semi speeding toward us.

THE SAMSON TRAP

At its core, Samson's trap represents a war that has been raging since the Fall. That war is defined by opposing forces wishing to control our hearts. On one side is the Lord Jesus Christ; on the other, the enemy of our faith. Both Jesus and Satan wish to influence the way we think and act. While the devil has our carnal nature to side with in the battle, Jesus joins us with his own Holy Spirit. Thus, the battle rages between what the flesh says it must have to survive in this world and what God's Holy Spirit suggests as an opposing survival tactic.

The Samson trap can be boiled down to the lies our sinful natures settle for in this regard—given that Satan is the father of lies. Those lies pertain to how we find lasting satisfaction for our weary souls. Usually, we end up believing that management through self-will is the best way to go. The Holy Spirit, on the other hand, invariably points us in the direction of heaven and the godly management of our souls' appetites.

Contentment is what we hunger for most. It keeps us going and makes our time spent on this earth worth the effort. Our Maker has wisely constructed within our souls a need to find a sense of acceptance, fulfillment, success, attachment, and worthwhile reward to truly be happy. Through these needs, he helps us to discover we can only find lasting satisfaction through life in him.

Only the Lord knows the way to lasting satisfaction for our hearts. It is a long, circuitous path chosen by him. It teaches us dependence on God while showing us that life's many frustrations are supposed to make one conclusion absolute in our minds: Jesus is the way to true contentment. He is the means by which God can guarantee we will be pleased with how things turn out in our lives (see Eph. 2:10).

In the process, we have the Samson trap to wrestle with. We're certain about what is going to make us happy—and we willingly take one wrong turn after another trying to prove it. We're determined to find peace of mind through self-help or whatever other strategy allows to stay firmly in the driver's seat.

FROM TRAPPED TO TRIUMPHANT

Samson is a noted figure of the Bible who demonstrated this nuance of human behavior rather well. He charged ahead without ever realizing how blind or empty he was. He also banked on "image" to get him by and refused to confront the fear that characterized his condition. That is why I have chosen him as the source of my look into what the Samson trap is all about. But his story doesn't end there. Samson's story offers the ray of hope we all need to get past our tendency to live in denial. Mostly by accident, Samson shows us the way around escapism and fear to a living faith in Jehovah God. Such faith represents the Lord's plan of salvation for all of us, for it is by his grace that we are saved through faith, not of ourselves (Eph. 2:8-9). Thank God!

Faith is the spiritual conduit by which God's Spirit and still, small voice become audible. It gives us access to the Lord's thoughts and gracious intentions toward us, usually coming by way of his Word revealed to our hearts (see Rom. 10:17).

The faith that our heavenly Father wishes to construct in our hearts is meant to fill the vacuum inside of us. It represents the return of the Holy Spirit to our lives, and it is carried out through the auspices of Jesus Christ. Faith in the resurrected Christ is the only prescription that works in assuaging our many fears. This is because Jesus wants to step into our hearts and take over our mis-directed lives. He wants to be our *everything,* the means by which sin and any sense of inadequacy are swallowed up through his perfect sufficiency.

Thus, it is with excitement that I invite you to study the life and times of Samson in order to find out all you can about the Samson trap. His story exemplifies what the Lord wants to do for all of us men in hiding. He wants to remove sin's blemish and transform us into the very likeness of his Son through a living faith in Jesus. Only then can we truly become "ex-cons" who discover that faking our way through life is no longer required for our survival. Jesus is the way and the truth and the life God intends for us—a life free of fear and full of promise. Hallelujah!

1

LOSING ONE'S HAIR

Why a book about Samson and the trap he fell into, you might ask? It is all about hair loss and the other things we men may lose along the way toward becoming spiritual adults. Loss has many things to teach us about life, the most important of which is that learning to trust in the Lord with all of our hearts is essential to our survival as men. Trusting in anything else to get by will likely lead to unnecessary heartache and our destruction.

Samson is a prime example of what hair loss can mean for a man. Scripture reveals that he lost his beautiful mane to a woman and became a spiritual has-been. However, his loss landed him in the arms of his Lord and Savior, whereby he came to his senses and regained his spiritual stature—just in the nick of time. My own story is not dissimilar.

ACHIEVING LIFE'S PERKS

I came to know the Lord in a rather circuitous manner. I started going to church mostly because a woman I was dating at the time said we should try it. I am sure it was guilt that drove us there: both of us had gone to church as youngsters, and our current sleeping arrangements were nagging at our respective consciences. Both of us knew what being slightly religious meant, yet neither of us knew anything about life in the Spirit. Consequently, going to church was meant to assuage our guilt and allow us to continue living in sin. At least, that's what we thought. God had other plans.

Throughout the course of early adulthood, I had become increasingly aware of my hair loss. Life with this woman now demanded I be concerned about such things. She impressed me as someone who was into image, but then so was I. Her history of quick romances told me she kept her eye open for any hunk who might come along. Consequently, by impressing her, I was proving what a prize I was. I was convinced that if I could just come up with the formula for the right look, she would be my perk for a while. Better yet, I could guarantee some "feel good" thoughts about myself if I liked what I saw staring back at me from the mirror each morning.

Sounds rather shallow, doesn't it? No surprise. I was living with the Samson trap around my neck. And that trap drove me to search out a solution for my poor self-image and my baldness in the open arms of medical science. The world of hair replacement was a vista of opportunity that leaped out at me from my newspaper every day. The sports section was filled with kindly looking doctors who smiled broadly below promising ad lines that suggested getting my hair back was only a matter of time and money. They would do the rest.

Hair transplants, implants, grafting techniques, suturing procedures, and other alternatives (even stapling) were wonderfully described, and they all seemed so simple. Hair was only one visit away for the interested consumer. From my point of view, money was no object. My appearance was worth the investment. So, too, was my dream of becoming an Adonis women wouldn't be able to resist.

SOLD OUT TO THE WRONG THINGS

What I didn't take into account was the fact that my appearance had little to do with the person I was. Fixing my hairline wasn't going to change my personality in any way or make me a better person. Smoking dope, sleeping with a woman to whom I wasn't married, and living life in the fast lane were all going to be part of my life after gaining the relief I sought. While my interest was on anything that would make me like myself more, God's desire was for me to like the person I was to become in Christ—someone sold out to the Lord. This person would finally be safe from the shills of this world who wanted my money and were willing to promise me the moon to get it.

I had decided I would try them all if it was necessary. It was. Each trip to the next treatment center only proved that nothing was going to replace my thinning hair. I tried suturing, grafting, and transplantation before I realized my head was beginning to look like a topographical map of the Rockies. Soon there were bumps and crevices everywhere. My increasingly scarred scalp indicated that being mortal (and increasingly imperfect) was my birthright. But I couldn't handle that thought. The desire to have hair outweighed any common sense. Thus, I subjected myself to one more procedure in order to achieve my ideal of human perfection.

An instrument with six needlelike prongs would be inserted into my scalp. Each prong carried with it a bundle of synthetic fibers that were left behind, under my skin, when the instrument was removed. Sounds awful, doesn't it? The Food and Drug Administration must have thought so. They ultimately outlawed the procedure. Nevertheless, I was in heaven when I saw hair starting to cover my head. After about two hours, I had the look I was after and left a satisfied customer.

WHEN DREAMS FALL SHORT

My head was now covered as much as my underlying shame over my faltering manhood. I rushed home to show off my new coif to my girlfriend. She seemed less than excited. What I didn't know was that she had been planning to leave me for some time, and now seemed about right to her. She said she needed a little more spice in her life. Sadly, my newly purchased masterpiece had no real impact on her. The world called and off she went.

The next bit of bad news was even more shattering. My hair was ditching me as well. Soon after the synthetic mane was combed into place, my scalp began reacting to the foreign objects embedded in it. I knew something was terribly wrong, but I had to place myself at the mercy of the same individuals who had carried out the madness in the first place. Their public relations man told me that sometimes the body reacts to foreign substances by trying to shed them through inflammation and a continuous pussy discharge. I needed prescription antibiotics, he explained, and then I would have to "wait and see." This uncertain diagnosis horrified me.

My ridiculous search for an honorable self-image had resulted in a degrading kind of dishonor. Samson was no different. He doggedly pursued an image that became his ruin. Maybe that is why his story has taken on such fascination for me. And the fact that he ultimately saw his hair removed certainly had significance for me. So, I began to search out any answers I could find on why such things happen and what their relevance might be for spiritual growth. In this regard, Samson has a good deal to teach all of us about what is important in this life and what isn't.

SAMSON'S BIRTH

Samson's story is told in the Old Testament book of Judges. Historically, we know that he was born between 1380 B.C. and 1050 B.C. Scripture tells us he was born to a childless Jewish couple in the land of Israel (Judg. 13–16). God announced to his parents that Samson would be a leader of his people and that he would bear witness to God's anointing on his life by being made a Nazirite. This religious order required its members to live a life of holy servitude to Jehovah God. Given that Samson's mother was barren, God's pronouncements were received with great joy. That joy didn't last long.

Once he got beyond his teen years, Samson showed the world that his time on earth was going to be spent doing devilish pranks rather than serving the Lord with all of his heart, soul, and mind.

Samson's biography is filled with drama. After reading it, even the casual observer will have to admit that the chronicle of Samson contains all the ingredients of a "must see" TV miniseries.

Samson was a stunning figure once he reached manhood. His physical stature was truly remarkable, and his military heroics hit the headlines every time he made sport of the enemy. This was a man who could do it all and had the muscles to prove it. The Bible tells us that Samson's strength was a gift from God. Spending all of his time at the gym or eating wheat germ had nothing to do with the awesome things he accomplished. Rather, the Lord empowered Samson in order to show the world what allegiance to his Spirit would mean for his people—victory over sin and darkness.

As a sign of Samson's willingness to remain a faithful servant to the Lord, Jehovah God asked that he never cut his hair. As long as a barber's shears never touched his glorious locks, Samson would be able to call upon the name of the Lord and carry out marvelous feats of strength. These included the routine slaughter of ferocious animals he encountered, as well as the destruction of Philistine garrisons in the area. As God's appointed champion, Samson fearlessly took on hundreds of enemy soldiers by himself. He seemed to be a man of steel who didn't require a cape. Some brains might have helped, though.

SAMSON'S WEAKNESS

Samson never got it through his thick head that his apparent invincibility was a measure of God's grace, or that the Lord wanted him to use his muscles exclusively against the enemy hordes enslaving his people. Instead, Samson saw his brawn as an excuse for showing off. Worse yet, he let his testosterone get the best of him, and he became a womanizer. Women meant more to him than a life of righteousness, evidenced by his compelling need to repeatedly fall in and out of lust. In the end, he tripped head over heels for a woman named Delilah, an enemy spy. His burning desire was to go to bed with her; her heart yearned for the moment she could hand him over to the Philistine army.

Once Samson achieved his desire, Delilah achieved hers. She cut off Samson's hair and he immediately lost his strength. Philistines then bound his hands and feet, poked out his eyes, and led him off to prison. To make matters worse, Samson experienced the loss of God's Holy Spirit as a companion and mentor. In an instant, Samson was made a nobody because he disavowed his allegiance to the Lord. Summarizing this tragic tale, a noted Bible teacher has said, "In his weakness, he got a haircut in the devil's barber shop and lost his power with God and influence with others."

Obviously, losing one's hair can truly be debilitating, if what we are speaking of has to do with the Lord's anointing. God wants to empower each of us through his Holy Spirit to face down the enemy. He wants the glory, of course, and we get the spoils. But we may not want to take God up on his offer. The world or our flesh may seem more inviting and off we go. Meanwhile, we may have to lose everything important to us in order to see that only the Lord's companionship guarantees meaning in our lives.

DESPERATE PEOPLE DO DESPERATE THINGS

As my hair began to fall out due to the progressing scalp infection, my heart took a nose dive. I felt abandoned by God as much as by my girlfriend. Out of sheer panic over my hair, I decided to make more frequent trips to the church up the street. I figured God would be impressed with my new "get serious" attitude. Besides, I assumed that if he was genuinely interested in me staying serious, he would give me my dearest wish: hair. It didn't even have to be the kind that grew. I would be just as pleased with the synthetic stuff I had paid for already. All God had to do was heal my scalp and everybody could go home happy.

To the reader all of this will sound terribly trite, I am sure. Yet, it describes the condition of my heart at the time I came to know the Lord. I was a man struggling with a male problem—and it wasn't baldness. It was the Samson trap. I was going to have to learn how to avoid it if I was ever going to learn to be anything more than a swindler to myself. Otherwise I would remain selfish, self-absorbed, and focused on getting my needs met any way I could.

Desperate people do desperate things, including permitting the Holy Spirit into their hearts. I gave my life to the Lord. As a result, I found myself crying over the brokenness of my heart and the destitution of my soul.

This life-changing event occurred during my season of trying to twist God's arm. I had started memorizing Scripture as a way of showing the Lord I meant business. Any Bible verse that held some promise for physical healing was offered up to God as a prayerful reminder that he had guaranteed such things to his believers. It didn't work. However, I was beginning to learn the Word of God. Soon the Lord was doing the arm twisting. He was allowing me to study the Bible for purely self-serving reasons and causing a change to take place nonetheless. My heart was softening to his invitation to let him come in and be my Lord and Savior.

Through all my scheming, God was showing himself to be sovereign in my life, just as his Word declares: "And we know that all things work together for good to those who love God, to those who are the called according to His purpose" (Rom. 8:28). In fact, out of chaos and frenzy would finally come divine order. The Lord was planning to write a happy ending to my lurid story, just as he did for Samson. Still, it would be his purposes that were served and not mine.

God desired for me to commit myself wholeheartedly to his lordship and enter into a dynamic and lifelong union with him. Hair wasn't very high on his list of those things that were purposed for my tenure on this earth. He knew a number of other things would prove to be more essential to my salvation, so my soul might be redeemed forever.

In particular, he needed me to see what had crippled me from birth. It was the Samson trap, and it served to keep me alone in my world and very much afraid.

A POLICY OF SURVIVAL

It is said that Israel has made a kind of national policy out of Samson's duress. Given the fact that the Jewish people were nearly destroyed as an ethnic group through the horrors of the Nazi holocaust, their government has articulated a policy of defense that will prevent such a travesty from ever occurring again. It is called the Samson Syndrome, and it calls for nuclear retaliation of the fullest measure if that nation's survival is ever threatened.

The fact this policy bears the name of the ancient Bible hero is no accident. Fears over the Jewish State's being exterminated by a hostile enemy is what has driven the government of Israel to seek out a solution that guarantees no compromise. They are determined to take as many of the bad guys with them as necessary, if another country is foolish enough to mess with them. This is just what Samson did at the end of his life.

Metaphorically speaking, ending up in a Philistine death camp was a fitting end to Samson's script. He had been held captive by something all of his life: fear. His antics throughout adulthood were simply a way of trying to cover up this fact. In psychology, we call this *compensation*. A man's bluster is usually a way of compensating for a deeper level of inadequacy. In Samson's case, apparent concerns over being seen as an average guy caused him to try and bulk up through a combination of brawn and promiscuity.

None of this helped Samson avoid the inevitable. He needed to find out that without a living and vibrant faith in God, he was just an average guy. Yes, Samson was a muscle man and could do wondrous things. But apart from the Holy Spirit, he wasn't going to get very far in this world, at least from an eternal perspective. The Lord wanted to be his true source of strength, holy compensation for his many human shortcomings. Sadly, Samson lost sight of this simple fact. In trying to prove himself worthy of the title "God's Golden Boy," he believed he could do it all, with no help from God. How wrong he was.

BRAVE ONCE MORE

Blind and bound, Samson decided that dying was the only way out
of the mess he found himself in. But he would not go alone. Placed
between two pillars in a Philistine dining hall, he summoned his
great strength one last time and pushed. By getting the pillars to
fall on top of him, Samson dropped the curtain on his life and
times—and he sent three thousand Philistines to their deaths.

For Samson, fear was not the last word in his biography. God
made him a very brave man at the end of his life. His bravery was
established through faith in his Lord. Samson decided to trust in
God to make the impossible happen, and it did. In this fashion, true
strength of character was fashioned within his soul and the world
saw what courage was all about.

Courage is never about bluster or baloney. It is about the Lord
bringing us to a place of faith in Christ Jesus through personal loss
and glaring insufficiency. Such faith allows us to fall miserably short
as humans and still see victory.

For this reason, Samson's demise parallels our own. We must
die to the idea that self-management of our lives (or our hairlines)
is going to work. Death of the human will is necessary if we are
ever to get beyond fear and find a living faith in the Lord. Only
then will our fractious lives make sense. Only then will we have
the kind of strength needed to make the world shake and temples
fall, all in the name of Jesus.

THINGS TO THINK ABOUT AND DO

The following exercises might prove helpful in beginning your journey from fear to faith in Christ. Keep a journal so you can record
your progress.

1. Read the story of Samson in its entirety in Judges 13–16. Write
   out your impressions as to what you think his character flaws
   might have been.

2. List ten ways you think you might be like Samson. Then try listing ten things you feel make you different from this Bible figure. Write a single paragraph in which you share how the story of Samson may help you grow spiritually.

3. List those things that represent areas of fear in your life and how they may hinder your walk of faith. Remember that we compensate when we are afraid, so look for areas in your life in which you compensate. Below the need to appear brave, strong, or unshakable may be the fear you are looking for. Write a prayer in which you talk about these fears and ask the Lord to deliver you from anything that keeps you afraid. Read this prayer daily for at least a week and make a journal entry as to how the Lord made you less afraid.

2

PROVING OUR MANHOOD

Important lessons on courage were still ahead for me. While God wanted me to walk in faith and not by sight (see 2 Cor. 5:7), getting around in the world seemed so much easier if I kept my eyes focused on myself. I was a man, after all, and looking my best ensured that I would be loved, no matter what my current girlfriend had decided to do. Besides, self-image had to be important; why else would God have allowed us to invent mirrors? Consequently, I was convinced that my sagging ego could be propped up by having hair.

Most of the miracle doctors had left town by now. I am sure they feared a lawsuit from all of us who had lined up in their waiting rooms. Everyone else's head was ablaze with infection just like mine. Sad to say, the clinic's nurses were left to attend to me and the others, and they offered little consolation. They dabbed at my wounds with antiseptics and told me to go home and wait a little longer.

Meanwhile, fear was becoming my constant companion. I had earnestly given the Lord my heart, so why wasn't he saving my hair? How else could I ever face the world again or have any hope of falling in love? If I looked like Frankenstein's monster, I would undoubtedly have to take up hiding in some colony outside the city gates.

DRIVEN TO FALSEHOOD

What would drive men toward such false beliefs? My lovely wife supplied the answer. You see, a woman did find me attractive enough to marry me—and a wonderful lady she is. But our paths didn't cross until the Lord was finished with his reconstruction project of my heart. He needed to replace the fear with a faith in something other than my flimflam appearance.

My wife's scenario of what makes men suckers to the world's ideas of greatness, charm, and the Schwarzenegger mystique was truly eye-opening for me. One evening she shared this thought: We men are born to be just like Samson. As we have seen, he was blinded by a need to appear invincible and was incapable of admitting his shortcomings. His downfall was made certain. My wife reasoned that, from birth, such a condition haunts all men and drives us to do the strangest things in order to save face.

Her hypothesis arose from recent experiences with our four year old, Joshua. His preschool teacher told us he was terrorizing children on the playground and acting generally bratty. Our hearts were torn between feeling angry over his misbehavior and feeling sorry for our little boy. We hadn't raised him to be a hellion; something was clearly wrong for him to be behaving this way.

When my wife asked Joshua what was wrong, he said he was afraid. When she inquired as to what was scaring him, he said he was afraid because "Mommy had gone away." Within moments of my wife's departure from his side on his first day at preschool, things had apparently started going dreadfully wrong with the other children. As kids will do, they started laughing at his clumsiness on the jungle gym. Joshua chose to play the tough guy from that point on. Pushing and shoving the other children became his way of hiding his self-consciousness. Moxie had replaced uncertain fears over his acceptability, as the Samson trap rose to the occasion.

Adult males are no different than my four-year-old son. We choose moxie over dread anytime we can get away with it. That's why Samson's story grabs our attention. He didn't seem to be afraid of anything, and we all wish we could say the same thing. We know that being men requires us to hold our heads high and appear unshakable.

DISCOVERING WE ARE NOT ALONE

My son was afraid because he felt alone. This same feeling characterized an inmate I worked with once, and moxie certainly became his solution. He told me he had always feared he couldn't count on anyone in this world. His father had left him and his mother when he was an infant. His mother had turned to drugs and men for solace. As he grew up, he learned to steal as a way of surviving because his mother was never around to take care of him. As a five year old, he had stolen a box of cereal from a local supermarket in order to have something to eat.

Things went from bad to worse, as the young man's heart hardened to the idea that no one cared. Below this jarring thought was the suspicion that he wouldn't survive unless he remained crafty in the art of outrunning the law. Grocery store shoplifting gave way to carjackings in his adult years, but the motive remained the same. Fear told him to thieve to get whatever he needed. Ironically, his own drug habit guaranteed he would go hungry anyway. Drugs demanded all of his earnings. He panhandled for food.

Interestingly enough, this man's heart was softened by an unexpected act of kindness. He recalled running into a stranger one morning on a street corner. This odd little man had offered to buy him breakfast if he was willing to hear about Jesus. He accepted the offer because he was hungry. After breakfast, this stranger invited him to church that evening for another free meal. The inmate told me he felt as though he couldn't say no.

Once at church, he felt strangely warm all over. In addition, he was absolutely shocked by the sense of acceptance he experienced from everyone in attendance. They embraced him and told him how happy they were he had decided to come. The sermon he heard told him of Jesus' love for him and how that love was expressed for all people on the cross at Calvary.

Surprisingly, the evening's last bit of business was the Lord's finishing touch. Small groups gathered together in the sanctuary for a foot-washing ceremony like the one offered by Jesus to his disciples on his last night with them. The same strange little man who had invited him bent down with a towel to wash his feet. In that moment, Jesus' love for him was made real.

In telling his tale, the inmate broke down and cried. He told me how much he had been struck by the revelation of God's heart toward him. In that moment he had finally begun to trust that someone cared and was there for him. Shortly after this church experience, he botched another carjacking and was arrested on the scene. He realized later that he had actually wanted to be caught in order to stop thieving. In jail, he accepted the Lord as his personal Savior.

NEEDING TO PROVE SOMETHING

As we will see, it is difficult for men to admit how empty they are. Trusting others is equally difficult. Pride plays a part in this quirk of our nature, but fear contributes something as well. Fear says that we must show ourselves capable, if we are going to prove we are men to begin with. Maybe, like my inmate friend, we are convinced no one is there for us. Or, maybe we have been raised thinking that crying was only for crybabies, so we learned to put on a tough exterior. In any case, asking for help is generally painful for us. Needless to say, this leads in the direction of the Samson trap.

If we look to Samson, we can see what the real problem is for all of us. It is a condition we carry in our soul, and it is called sin. In reading the first lines of the Bible story of Samson, we can begin to understand what I mean. Verse one of the Judge's account tells us: "Again the children of Israel did evil in the sight of the Lord, and the Lord delivered them into the hand of the Philistines for forty years" (Judg. 13:1). In one line, we discover the root cause of the Samson trap: the need to go our own way.

In the case of the ancient Hebrews, they set out to prove they could find national contentment without any help from God. God had warned his people shortly after their exodus from Egypt that such things would be coming up in their collective conscious. He shared with their spokesperson, Moses, that he was ready to lead them into a land of promise, yet something would stand in their way. By his foreknowledge, the Lord warned Moses that fear would tell the Israelites the Lord couldn't be trusted, and rebellion would lead them in the wrong direction. Heading back out into the desert would somehow make more sense than relying on the Lord.

Their ultimate turnaround was carried out in spite of the Lord's promise: "If you walk in My statutes and keep My commandments, and perform them, . . . I will give peace in the land, and you shall lie down, and none will make you afraid" (Lev. 26:3-6). They didn't get it.

AFRAID TO THE VERY CORE

How could they have been so dumb? Well, frankly, we're no different, thanks to our sin nature. At our core, we're afraid because we have taken on a corruptible nature. As Pastor Charles Neiman has noted, "Fear is a spiritual force, and it is a powerful force. With fear in your heart, the Word of God will not work."

Originally, we were created in God's image and made perfect in every way. But, with the fall of man in the Garden of Eden, we have taken on a different image (see Gen. 3). In part, that image includes fearfulness.

Moral and spiritual destitution resulted from Adam and Eve's disobedience. They chose to disobey God and spiritual wholeness was lost forever. A painful self-consciousness settled into Adam and Eve's hearts. It caused them to see their nakedness (the bad stuff) and turn way. They wrongly presumed they couldn't count on God any longer and they would have to survive on their own. Does this sound familiar?

Fear compelled our progenitors to hide themselves with fig leaves and avoid each other. Worst of all, they took up hiding from God.

In his own words, Adam shared something with God on behalf of all of us: "I heard your Voice in the garden, and I was afraid because I was naked; and I hid myself" (Gen. 3:10).

An internal unrest told Adam and Eve they were deficient in their natural state (which they were) and needed to learn to cover up their shallowness and sin. The age of pretense had arrived. The need for cover-ups suggested that pointing the finger at the other guy would somehow help. In this spirit, they began casting aspersions and accusations, blaming each other for their own weaknesses. Rather than trying to be honest, they began excusing themselves; sincerity between the sexes was lost forever. Meanwhile, honesty with God was pitched out. Fear was behind it all.

FIG LEAVES WILL NEVER DO

Unfortunately, fear is now endemic to the human race, thanks to an unremitting sin nature. Our sinfulness tells us we are eternally separated from God, while fear says we must strike out on our own to survive in a cruel and unjust world. Insecurities about such things dwell disguised deep within our hearts and must be eradicated as much as our sin. After all, our many fears are intertwined with every frailty we learn to live with as Samson's counterparts. Such trepidations spawn the deceit we use to shroud our mistakes. They fuel the contempt we feel over everybody else's success.

Fear is surely the plight of men of the church today. We fear being seen as less spirit filled or underweight in terms of our spiritual diet, so we take up hiding. Our world of "churchianity" dictates we talk a certain talk and walk a certain walk, so no one is left thinking we aren't the believers we need to be. These shenanigans are all cover-ups.

God supplied Adam and Eve with animal hides to replace their fig leaves, and symbolically their sins and obvious shortcomings were remedied. God needed them to see that being spiritually whole once more would require a good deal more than their ability to "make do." They needed to have a living faith in someone besides themselves. God's promise to them in that moment was to send them a Savior to deliver them from certain doom (see Gen. 3:15). He made subtle reference to this Savior's future sacrifice by sacrificing an innocent beast in the Garden for Adam and Eve's new apparel. This animal sacrifice pointed to what the Lord would ultimately offer all of humanity. On the cross, God's sacrificial Lamb and only Son, Jesus, was crucified to pay the price for our sin: "For He made Him who knew no sin to be sin for us, that we might become the righteousness of God in Him" (2 Cor. 5:21).

Through Jesus, we have an opportunity to return to a state of spiritual being that parallels our original wholeness. The Lord supplies a living faith to our hearts aimed at letting Jesus become the center of our lives. Through him, we don't have to pretend we can make it on our own any longer. Falsehood can cease while our sins are washed away and our underlying fears are abated. The faith God has purposed for our lives is based on the truth of who Jesus is as our once-and-for-all sacrifice. God knows that fig leaves will never do, so he sent Jesus into the world to save us from sin, darkness, and ourselves.

Such salvation includes being released from our bondage to fear. In fact, God guarantees we will become more than conquerors in Christ (Rom. 8:37). In the process, the Spirit of Jesus comes to dwell within our hearts. He gains our freedom from the Samson trap as we come to a place of rest in him. The age of cover-ups is over at last.

DEFINING FEAR AND FAITH

Nevertheless, fear stands in the way of such an overhaul. While our salvation is achieved the moment we decide to let Jesus come into our hearts, our fearful spirits aren't rectified immediately. We remain timid creatures who find trusting in the Almighty a difficult task indeed. He is invisible, after all, and we are so used to doing things by sight, not by faith.

Secular practitioners understand the role fear plays in the lives of every human being. James Masterson has suggested that this search for the real self is the underlying task we all face in trying to become psychologically whole. The *real self* is a person relatively free of fear. On the other hand, Masterson postulates that the *false self* becomes the predominating part of us when we suffer any kind of significant setback in our emotional lives as children. This persona is incapable of being honest about himself or his shortcomings because of his need to hide. His self-worth will be so reduced that he will be capable only of defending himself against exposure of his many inadequacies.

Given that so much can go wrong for us emotionally, fear is bound to follow. Faith in Christ is the only thing that can get us past our original sin nature and the fear that characterizes humanity. Consequently, I have come up with a working definition of what fear and faith look like, so we can recognize them when they knock at our emotional door—and choose wisely between them.

F = Fixating on our problems

E = Escaping into fantasy or the easy way out

A = Avoiding God's remedies and choosing our own

R = Retreating into pretense

F = Facing frustration with hope

A = Acknowledging God knows what he is doing

I = Inviting the Holy Spirit into every situation

T = Trusting that God will come through for you

H = Holding on to God's promises, no matter what

I realize the attitudes and behaviors that define faith will take a lifetime to implement. Not to worry, because God will supply whatever is needed (see Heb. 4:16). However, we can help. First, facing frustration with hopeful expectation means not letting circumstances frighten us into believing God has disappeared. We need to turn to the Bible and look for reasons for encouragement.

Next, acknowledging God's know-how boils down to assuming God has everything scoped out. We can remind ourselves of this important fact by making a list of all the times he has come through for us in the past. If that doesn't work, make a list of the times he came through for his people in their desert wanderings. (Read the Old Testament book of Exodus.) Trusting God with the outcome for any situation means learning to rest with the idea that things will turn out okay, no matter how they look right now. When afraid, try writing a letter thanking God (in faith) for how things will turn out.

Finally, holding onto God's promises means reminding ourselves that Jesus died on the cross for us; anything needed in our current situation will be provided by him. Nothing is too difficult for him. When in doubt, try repeating this Bible verse to yourself throughout the day: "With God all things are possible" (Matt. 19:26).

THINGS TO THINK ABOUT AND DO

1. Make a list of Bible verses that address the issue of God's faith-fulness. Find those verses that speak to your heart about God's desire to protect you and preserve your faith. Practice memoriz-ing one verse a day until you have memorized your entire list. Then, try writing them down from memory. Now you are equipped in the Spirit to face fear with a sword that is able to cut through any lies about your safety or well-being (see Heb. 4:12).

2. Try coming up with your own definition of faith and writing it in your journal. Pray that God will give you this kind of faith. Go to a Christian bookstore or your church library and find a book on the subject of faith that interests you, and read it. (But promise me you will finish the book you're currently reading first!)

3. In what ways have you seen fear and rebellion going hand-in-hand in your life? Describe those times and write out your thoughts about how you would handle those situations now, as a more mature believer in Christ.

3

THE SPIRITUAL STARTING POINT

Everything we set out to do in this life requires we begin at a starting point. Achieving a life of faith is no different. It requires we find the proper starting point, which I call Point A. This point is a place of small beginnings, a place where we discover that frustration is our spiritual starting point. Learning to handle frustration is the only means for growing in the faith. In fact, as we travel the distance from fear to faith, frustration represents the major itinerary along the way. That's as it should be.

Samson's mother certainly discovered the utility of frustration in finding her way along a path of faith. Undoubtedly, her infertility would have been a source of exasperation and discontent. After all, every Jewish bride hoped to be the mother of the promised Messiah. In addition, being barren was typically seen as a kind of curse resulting in a sense of stigma, both socially and spiritually. The prospect of having to face life as an "incomplete woman" would have compelled her to look to God for any answers that might soothe her troubled soul.

God used her languishing heart and fervent anticipation to make her receptive to a message he wanted to send her way. Her endless waiting caused her to be all ears. An angel was dispatched from heaven with word that she would soon be pregnant and the new arrival would be no ordinary child: "You shall conceive and bear a son," the angel said. "No razor shall come upon his head, for the child shall be a Nazirite to God from the womb; and he shall begin to deliver Israel out of the hand of the Philistines" (Judg. 13:5).

FRUSTRATION'S DIVIDENDS

Samson's mother was ready to listen. This is undoubtedly the first real dividend of frustration—we develop a capacity for listening. Frustration tells us that our plan, whatever it may have been, isn't working. God's plan is made so much easier to accept after life and all of our self-help books have deposited us at the end of our ropes.

Frustration also compels us to finally let the Lord be sovereign in our lives. In giving up on ourselves, the lordship of Jesus Christ becomes a must. Who else do we have to lean on? In truth, we are all barren (spiritually speaking) until the Lord's sovereignty is established in our hearts. This profound truth was stated eloquently by King David, who wrote, "But I am poor and needy; make haste to me, O God! You are my help and my deliverer; O Lord, do not delay" (Ps. 70:5). However, such an admission usually doesn't come until frustration has had its way with us first.

Being at our wits' end has many things to teach about faith. It tells us we can't afford to be too pigheaded about how our faith is going to get constructed and when. Getting to Point B can only be assured if we choose to let the Lord show us the way. Characteristically, Samson was going to have to find this out the hard way. While he would initiate a plan of action for the rescue of God's people from the Philistines, he would trip over his own big feet and lack of faith.

WE ARE TO BE HOLY

By divine appointment, Samson's sojourn on earth was supposed to be carried out in righteous service to the Most High God. He was declared a Nazirite from birth. Such a proclamation required Samson to "separate himself to the Lord" (see Num. 6:2). *Separation* meant a life of purity and commitment was ahead of him, starting at his birth. There wasn't going to be much time for high jinks along the way.

All believers are called to a similar pursuit of holiness. We are to be holy as God is holy (see Lev. 11:44). Again, we hear frustration tapping its foot, wanting God to explain. It seems too difficult a task. How could God be so demanding? The good news is that the Lord fully intends to fashion an earnestness within our souls that is lifelong and pointed directly at him. He accomplishes this through hard times, along with the ministration of his grace in response to each and every cry for help. As we come to realize that holiness can only be dispensed from a throne room where unconditional love abounds, we can breathe a little easier. Thankfully, human effort has nothing to do with how our faith gets constructed.

I had much to learn in this regard. I assumed God was the good-luck charm I had been seeking. His sovereignty was of much less concern to me than getting him to give into my ideas about what male virility was all about. I had much to tell him about how my problems in this area could best be handled. Far past frustrated, I figured the Lord just didn't see the effect all of this was having on me.

How could I really worship the Lord, if the whole time I was in church I obsessed over my appearance? How could I really believe his Word, if God didn't seem to live up to what he said in Scripture? How could I tell others about the Lord, if I was too busy hiding from the world because I felt so ugly? These questions seemed legitimate and I needed some answers. None were forthcoming though.

RUDELY AWAKENED

As a baby Christian, I was in for a rude awakening. I had to realize that I would need to move over into the passenger seat and let God take over my life. What took so long for that lesson to sink in? For one thing, I clearly wasn't at the end of my rope yet. There were too many things I whined about (spiritually speaking) if I didn't get my way.

Meanwhile, I tried my best to impress the Lord. I wrongfully concluded that if the Lord could see my spiritual life taking on a polish and sheen that would blind the average Christian, he would be impressed. Then, he would grant my wish for hair. My attitude would carry me right to the top of the corporate ladder in God's glorious kingdom. Obviously, I needed to see that God doesn't hand out merit badges or advancement notices to his employees. He rewards all of his children equally for he has no favorites.

For most of us, fear doesn't let us see this aspect of God's character right away. Insecurity tells us that the world is slowly spinning down and we have only one shot at becoming something more than ordinary. Therefore, collecting prizes (or improving our lot) becomes our solution, no matter who is running the show. If God is in charge of this universe, then we'll just have to find out what his benefit package looks like. Surely we can expect some kind of incentive plan for getting ahead—or at least compensation for working overtime.

This brand of self-delusion is brought with us from the world into God's kingdom. It certainly reflects the reward system we have set up for ourselves on earth. Thankfully, the Lord wants nothing to do with it. So once more God lifts frustration from his toolbox and puts it to use. If we are trying to please the Lord as a way of manipulating him, we can forget it. It doesn't work and will only leave us more frustrated. We cannot earn what God has chosen to give freely: his love and forgiveness.

Even so, I went to as many Bible studies as I could find in the church brochure. I loaned three hundred dollars to a woman who said she needed it; I never saw the money again. Later, I coughed up a check for several thousand dollars to a television evangelist whose ministry seemed worthy. All of my giving was predicated on the notion that God loves a cheerful contributor and probably wants to reward him or her in some way.

At the same time, I stood in front of a mirror nearly every day for more hours than I want to admit, hoping to see my infections subside. They didn't. God would have nothing to do with my need to earn an A in a course for which I had received a passing mark already, thanks to Jesus. Hair was simply not going to be the Lord's way of congratulating me on my hard work or spiritual overachievement. Salvation was mine already and anything else I might truly need would be given as a gift from the Lord.

THE INNER MAN IS BLIND

Samson's father was a bird of a similar feather whose approach to such things was not unlike my own. When his wife told him the tale of an angelic messenger, Manoah didn't really trust it. Reading between the lines, we can venture a guess why. Perhaps he thought God would have delivered the news in a more respectable way. Perhaps he thought God would have delivered it to him, not his wife. In any case, he insisted he would have to hear from the Lord himself in order to draw his own conclusions (Judg. 13:8-18).

This brand of religious delusion arises because, by himself, the inner man is incapable of seeing where he is heading. He is totally blind and definitely needs the Holy Spirit's assistance in finding his way to Point B. After all, God's strategies for constructing a life-changing trust in him are seldom what we would have dreamed up on our own: " 'For My thoughts are not your thoughts, nor are your ways My ways,' says the Lord," the prophet Isaiah wrote (Isa. 55:8).

As frustration would have it, we newborn Christians often travel in broad circles in trying to procure such faith on our own. We don't allow the Holy Spirit to educate us on how to appropriate God's blessings through faith; it takes time and effort. Consequently, Point A (where faith begins) and Point B (where fear leaves off) don't exist in our minds and no straight line can be drawn between them.

Out of ignorance, we assume that being a Christian means things will be rosy from now on. Not true. Or we come to the conclusion that God will consult us on most things before he does anything drastic in our lives. Equally not true.

Our notions about issues of faith are all wrong. Remember, they're based on fear and lead to frustration. Glory be to God! He can use every bit of our frustration to his purposes. God's path toward a living faith was intended to be bewildering. Forget about straight lines. The Lord has always had something more curvilinear in mind. He knew this was the only way to stay two steps ahead of our scheming and highly overachieving hearts.

GOD'S PRESCRIPTION

Just in case we miss the obvious, God makes sure we learn what life is meant to teach us. Life's major object lesson is that looking in God's direction is a must. That is where frustration comes in handy. Frustration helps us begin to develop the spiritual eyes and muscle that make our journey to Point B successful. We won't get lost along the way, if we keep on the lookout for Jesus. Meanwhile, consternation will surely make us true muscle men in God, because we will learn to go to him for everything.

The apostle Paul wrote, "We also glory in tribulations, knowing that tribulation produces perseverance; and perseverance, character; and character, hope" (Rom. 5:3-4). Jack Hayford, who has helped spearhead the men's movement in the United States, has described what the Lord is able to work in us through hard times. In his book *A Man's Walk with God,* he suggests that by the time the Lord is finished with us, an ordinary man will become God's extraordinary man; a fearful man will find God's power; a stumbling man will find sure footing; a growing man will learn God's priorities; a questioning man will learn holy certainty; and, an imperfect man will be transformed through God's perfecting power. Thus, it seems all the screaming and hollering in our spirits may be worth it, no matter how frustrated we become in striving for faith.

My call to faith was very much in front of me, along a path that made no sense. Frustration would get me there mostly out of desperation as I sought the Lord for answers. God's work in my life demanded I scrutinize something more troubling than my scalp: the attitude behind my attempt to possess hair in the first place. What was that attitude? I sincerely believed I could do anything on my own. I just needed God for the incidentals.

The world reinforced that message, preaching it in all those alluring ads for hair replacement, liposuction, and whatever else was offered toward self-improvement. All I needed was money—and the next technological advance promising "feel good" thoughts could be mine. Mercifully, the Lord knew my self-image was being built out of Lincoln Logs. He would have nothing to do with it.

A Good Work Is Begun

Falsehood needed to be replaced with vision for what God wished to accomplish for me. Spending my "todays" mesmerized by ads or mirrors would only frustrate me more. They could tell me only one thing: I was getting older, no doubt about it. Baldness was just the beginning. If I focused on the externals, I'd soon have a long list of changes to fret over. Instead, I had to learn to see the invisible: the person God was creating me to be beyond today. Only then would I begin to trust that happiness could truly be mine, because "He who has begun a good work in you will complete it until the day of Jesus Christ" (Phil. 1:6). God assures us that the outcome will be good. It's just going to take a while.

When we come to the end of our rope, we have to reach out to God. He is ready with a helping hand. By default, our hearts are made ready to embrace the Lord's promises for our deliverance. Hello, trust; good-bye, fear. This is why my bad days outweighed the good in the early weeks of faith. I had to learn to look beyond circumstance to see how I was doing in my Father's sight.

The Lord has provided the lasting solution for endless self-reflection by way of Christ's atoning sacrifice on the cross. God's readiness to forgive all of our sins and failures allows us to be confident in his care; the ads on the sports page simply become part of yesterday's news, not the last hope for a new hairline. Since we are no longer being graded on our ability to perform for our Maker, we can be certain of getting all the way to Point B without the worry. Frustration becomes obsolete. Paul put it succinctly by saying that God "chose us in Him before the foundation of the world, that we should be holy and without blame before Him in love" (Eph. 1:4).

Finally, we can see the line God has in mind. The shortest distance between Points A and B is a line of mercy and grace, where we can afford to be sinful and still find forgiveness for our sins. Holiness is guaranteed, no matter what. That doesn't mean we give up trying to do our best as Christians; it means we can surely give up worrying about what God thinks of us. And if he ain't going to complain, why should anyone else's opinion (or even our own) count for so much? Toss that mirror out and learn to smile at life's frustrations. Heaven is just ahead.

MOVING ON

To this end, the Lord had to thoroughly exasperate me. My infected scalp didn't get better. It got worse. Another trip to the doctor's office was looming. All the while, I knew God was my only hope of escaping the shame of being imperfect. The world's prescriptions hadn't worked.

I began to understand all of this as church attendance became a joy and not an artful ploy to get God to listen. I actually started to feel God's presence and sense his approval through the believers I met there. The fact that the strangers I encountered looked beyond the bandages covering my head and asked no embarrassing questions left me feeling safe. Their willingness to befriend me was even more encouraging.

In addition, I was beginning to grow in the faith by learning how to use the Bible in a manner that was not so self-serving. I no longer spent all of my time looking up God's promises about healing. Through the Bible studies I attended, friendship deepened into fellowship in the Spirit. I discovered God's Word was spirit and life and could be counted on to show me how to survive each day with the knowledge that God had everything under control.

Most excitedly, I learned that the Bible is a kind of travel log or map on our journey toward faith. It helps us overcome fear as we begin to see the distance that must be traveled and the kind of faith required to reach our final destination. It assures us we can travel the whole path between Point A (our new birth) and Point B (a living faith in Christ) by learning to trust in the Lord one day at a time. That's all the bigger our faith ever needs to be.

So, let's have a peek at the map God has provided for all of us journeymen. The Bible is chock-full of interesting tidbits about the route God has envisioned for us, in moving us from fear to faith. It looks like this:

A MAP OF SPIRITUAL MATURITY

Point A: Features of Spiritual Newborns	Point B: Features When Spiritually Mature
Easily stressed	Has lasting peace (Rom. 5:1)
Overactive	Can be still (Ps. 139:17-18)
Egocentric	Serves others (Gal. 5:13)
Immature	Spiritually minded (Eph. 4:23)
Demanding	Always content (Phil. 4:11)
Easily fatigued	Has strength (Phil. 4:13)
Messy	Remains spotless (2 Pet. 3:14)
Requires soft food	Chews solids (Heb. 5:14)
Easily distracted	Stays grounded (Eph. 3:17)
Full of mischief	Walks blamelessly (Prov. 28:18)
Lacks self-control	Shows self-control (2 Tim. 2:4)
Unable to stand	Able to withstand (Eph. 6:13)
Lacks an identity	Knows his name (Isa. 61:6)
Grabs everything	Able to resist (James 1:12)
Frustrates easily	Doesn't give up (2 Tim. 4:7)
Needs a diaper change	Cleansed of sin and shame (Rom. 8:1)
Lacks good judgment	Judges things rightly (1 Cor. 2:15)
Lacks knowledge	Has knowledge (2 Pet. 1:5-6)
Lacks initiative	Shows the way (1 Tim. 4:12)
Always needs help	Provides help (2 Cor. 1:4)

THINGS TO THINK ABOUT AND DO

1. Make a list of things that have seemingly gone wrong for you since becoming a Christian. Admit you're frustrated by them and ask the Lord to reveal to you what purpose is served in your frustration. Then write out the ways these things may help to make you stronger in your faith.

2. List those items from the Map of Spiritual Maturity that represent where you think you are in your walk with the Lord. Look to the Point A side of the list to see where you have begun your journey, and ask yourself how far you have to go to get to Point B. Write down your feelings about this. Try to identify the personality qualities you know God would like to change.

3. Next, write a prayer to the Lord asking him to make those changes a reality. Keep a daily log to see what changes the Lord brought about for you today, or in what way you tried to be more mature in Christ during the day.

4. How is your self-image built of Lincoln Logs? List those things about your appearance, your performance, or your ability to please others that seem essential for feeling okay about yourself. Then take the list and show it to a friend and ask him or her to pray for you as you try surrendering each item, one at a time. Let your friend know how you are doing.

4
TAKING THE
SAMSON TEST

Sooner or later we learn that our life in Christ places us on a path where the inevitable runs into the unavoidable. The inevitable habits we have established for getting by in the world run straight up against God's desire for us to turn them over to him. "Out with the old; in with the new" becomes God's next challenge to us as we venture deeper into the realm of faith.

We don't know for certain that Samson's mother was trapped by any nasty habits (otherwise known as compulsions), but for good reason the Lord admonished her to avoid drinking or eating anything unhealthy from now on (Judg. 13:7). Abstention was a visible sign that she was ready to hand over her soul's care to the Lord as part of the Nazirite code of behavior. Such a code (or vow) comes under the heading of divine conscription. Conscription of this sort involves the Lord's asking the believer to hand over some behavior, so he or she might see there is life after death, even the death of the human will.

By getting any of us to give up an old lifestyle, God introduces us to the hope that does not disappoint, as God's love is poured into our frightened hearts (see Rom. 5:5). The Lord accomplishes this important task through the power of his Holy Spirit. He tells us what he wants from us and then provides assistance as needed through the Spirit's comfort and peace.

Jesus told all of us how to grasp the idea that faith requires we move beyond our habitual way of surviving. He rightfully challenged our perception of such things by stating: "You did not choose Me, but I chose you and appointed you that you should go and bear fruit, and that your fruit should remain, that whatever you ask the Father in My name He may give you" (John 15:16). As hard as it is to believe, we have been appointed to live fruitful lives. We can surrender our addictions—no matter what they may be. We simply need to ask God to begin his work of recovery in us.

ARE YOU LISTENING, GOD?

An all-important lesson on conscription began for me the day I returned to the clinic to have my head examined. (Boy, did I need my head examined!) The physicians looked me over and agreed about one thing: my synthetic hair had to come out. Dejectedly, I watched as the medical team began the gruesome job of removing the implants, strand by bloody strand.

I was being plucked like a chicken, and I felt frozen inside. I kept thinking about my new relationship with the Lord and wondered what else the future would hold for me as a new believer.

For one thing, I felt "stood up" by the Lord. Since I knew God wasn't deaf, I considered other reasons for his inaction. And slowly I realized that the mess I was in stemmed from fearful thoughts I had been trying to escape for a long time. I began to understand my primary motivation in life had always been one of hiding my many deficiencies away.

With this thought in mind, God kept sticking the world's shortcomings in my face. Since the world offered ready-made solutions for all my fearful thoughts about self, God had to make certain none of them worked anymore. He wanted me to deal with feelings of deficiency that were as old as I was. The problem was they were safely out of view, due to a good deal of emotional topsoil and the blinding glitz of Madison Avenue's best marketing efforts. In this regard, my imperfections were neatly hidden beneath an expensive, synthetic nightmare.

THE SECRET OF INADEQUACY

Compulsions of most kinds arise to convince ourselves that we're not going to be exposed anytime soon. They help us keep our feelings of inadequacy a secret through emotional deception. We hold on to any number of habits or brainless ideas that make us feel better for now.

As is the case with all of us, feelings of inadequacy were pervasive for me for many reasons. Being the second born of two boys meant I had to live in the shadow of someone who was older and wiser. My brother always seemed to gain my father's approval because he could do things "right." All the while, my father was emotionally aloof, which made it nearly impossible to get him to notice me. My mom's love felt generally unavailable as well. She seemed plagued by a sadness that caused crying jags and suggested she had problems of her own.

Each of us has a similar story to tell. We have a knapsack of "second thoughts" slung over our shoulders. These insecurities arise in realizing that the love and comfort we hunger for will never be achieved and for good reason. Our parents undoubtedly faced life in the midst of their own pain and tried to meet our needs as children by way of their own insecurities. In truth, they were only human, bound to fail in meeting the needs only a divine Benefactor could satisfy. So we believe that our many unmet needs will simply remain that way. All the while, fear convinces us that it's up to us to meet those needs we have to make it on our own. Any feelings of inadequacy get tucked away; they would only remind us we're not making it after all.

Such fears were pervasive for me. Growing up as the kid in the family, I wasn't expected to be much help around the house. I could go off and play when something had to be done. But I also grew up believing I just wasn't wanted by my parents. When I needed comfort, I turned to my brother, who was five years older and something of a father figure to me. He was always willing to help me.

When my brother left home for college, I remember feeling angry at a picture of Jesus that hung in our bedroom. Life had suddenly become highly unpredictable. How could I survive without an older brother to protect me? To make matters worse, that picture seemed to mock me. Jesus' presence taunted me with the thought that he was only there to watch, not necessarily lend a hand.

DEFICIENCY MOTIVATED

Noted psychologist Abraham Maslow saw the achievement of human potential as dependent on one's ability to gratify certain interpersonal needs. Maslow noted five major needs shared by all human beings moving toward something he called self-actualization. This "hierarchy of needs" included physical needs, safety needs, security needs, needs for a sense of belonging, and finally self-esteem needs. Presumably, if all these needs are gratified, we become "self-actualized" and capable of standing on our own emotionally. If these go unmet, Maslow theorized that we become "deficiency motivated." We begin operating out of hunger and desperation as we get stuck in our emotional growth. We never feel complete, incapable of being all grown up.

Obviously, we carry around a tremendous potential for fear; seeing our needs go unmet, we must admit our infantile nature. When life gets the best of us, we become more and more deficiency motivated and afraid. To make matters worse, we won't want to admit that we're insufficient—it seems unmanly. Rather, believing that fear only characterizes the other guy, we go on trying to show the world our Superman routine. Compulsions help us live out the fiction.

Fears of all kinds tell us we don't count and nobody cares. A fretful brand of self-talk is with us until Jesus arrives to offer another opinion. Ultimately, he is able to convince us that our lot in

life isn't just a quick turn on the merry-go-round. His personal sacrifice on the cross leaves no room for doubt about such things, even
in our skeptical hearts. Still, Jesus isn't able to sell us on this point
right away. Exchanging an outdated thought life for something new
and closer to the truth takes time.

I was certain that the feelings of aloneness I carried in my soul
were mine for keeps. I was just passing through this world gaining
evidence that no one cared. There was nothing to which I could
cling for a sense of well-being, except my beautiful hair. The Lord
very patiently had to show me that there was a scared little boy
beneath my vain attempts at looking good. He gently revealed to
me that all my idiosyncrasies regarding my appearance had to do
with fears over being mortal, alone, and amounting to nothing. By
recognizing this fact, I was able to move beyond death's grip on
my soul and experience freedom.

This is accomplished for each of us when God shows us there
is life after death through the power of conscription. In essence,
the Lord shows us that we can survive without certain habits and
experience true happiness. All we have to do is die to the impulse
to grab life's pleasures or give into the one thing we know is slowly
killing us. Such healthy dying begins the moment we recognize that
remaining deficiency motivated makes no sense. Instead, Christ
guarantees that we can be motivated by his presence and know the
fullness of his Spirit instead.

THE SAMSON TEST

Compulsions undoubtedly characterize each of us, but getting beyond them is essential. To accomplish this, we must see the fear
that fuels their continued presence. To help, I have constructed
something I call the "Samson Test." It can help define the trap of
fear Samson made so famous.

THE SAMSON TEST

Answer true or false to each of the following statements. Be as honest as possible.

1. When I'm not looking my best, I'm "bugged."   T   F
2. When I goof up, I get down on myself.   T   F
3. When people disapprove of me, I get mad at them
   or myself.   T   F
4. When people approve of me, I don't necessarily believe
   what they're saying.   T   F
5. When I'm with a crowd, I feel I have to stand out in
   some way. Otherwise, I'll try to become invisible.   T   F
6. When somebody is watching, I get nervous about how
   I'm "doing."   T   F
7. When I've given in to my favorite habit, I always feel
   like I need more.   T   F
8. When I'm having fun, I start thinking about what else I
   can do to have more fun.   T   F
9. When I want to have a good time, I need to be around
   people who can let down their hair and be slightly
   reckless.   T   F
10. When I want to let loose, I have to get a little "crazy."   T   F
11. When people don't see what I want from them, or my
    needs are not met right away, I get angry.   T   F
12. When I'm feeling edgy, doing something compulsive
    helps (for example, eating, drinking, having sex, or
    climbing Mt. Everest).   T   F
13. When I've been put down or slighted, I feel hurt and
    I think about getting even.   T   F
14. When I'm in control of things, I feel good.   T   F
15. When I don't know how to do something, I fake my
    way through without asking for help.   T   F

16. When I'm down, I think I'm just feeling sorry for myself.   T   F
17. When I play a game, I feel like I have to win.   T   F
18. When I feel like I'm not getting my point across, I end up yelling or breaking something.   T   F
19. When I'm alone, I get bored and resort to self-stimulation—pornography helps in this regard.   T   F
20. When someone says they care, I want proof.   T   F
21. When I'm tired, I usually turn on the TV and channel surf.   T   F
22. When I am feeling affectionate, getting physical seems essential.   T   F
23. When I try reading the Word, I end up daydreaming.   T   F
24. When people tell me I've disappointed them, I stop listening. I figure I just have to be me and they'll have to get used to it. Besides, life is too short to worry about all this.   T   F
25. When I'm in a relationship, I invariably start thinking about what I have contributed versus what I have gotten in the deal.   T   F
26. When I feel like rewarding myself, something slightly extravagant usually fills the bill.   T   F
27. When I'm out with friends for dinner, I quickly figure out who paid the last time.   T   F
28. When I do something nice, I want people to say thank-you.   T   F
29. When I give up something, I think about what I might get in return.   T   F
30. When I get a gift, I usually think about other things I wanted more.   T   F

OUR SPIRITUAL NEEDS

In chapter 6 we will go into a more detailed evaluation of your responses here. For now, we will see how the Samson Test defines the inner man by showing how fear manifests itself. It reflects a range of responses we offer on our own behalf to meet certain basic needs. These needs are intrinsic to our new nature in Christ and can be categorized in a manner similar to Maslow's hierarchy. Each need represents an inherent desire to know something about our newly established life in Christ. Collectively, they involve how we face the major issues of our lives as eternal beings. Clearly, if any one of these needs goes unmet, our sense of well-being will be affected.

In general, our five major spiritual needs are represented by the following:

1. Acceptance. The first need evolves out of the uncertainty we feel over our acceptability as spiritual beings. Our awareness of being solitary figures in a frightening world is immediate from birth. Beyond this, feelings of hurt and rejection never seem far away. After all, getting swatted on the backside upon delivery tells each of us all we have to know about how things are going to be from now on. Upon our new birth, our spirits begin the search for eternal security. Acceptance has to be established in our hearts in order for us to be willing to face life and the hereafter wholeheartedly.

2. Fulfillment. Once we are born again, we experience a need to find lasting fulfillment for our souls. Such fulfillment is important for answering the question of why we exist. In the absence of contentment, life quickly becomes a drag, and we start feeling like mere accidents. Thus, a desperate attempt begins toward making life a generally positive experience. If we fail in our attempt, sheer exhaustion (from so much worry) convinces us that satisfaction just isn't our birthright, and the Creator never really cared all that much.

3. Success. Since men are typically "doers," achievement becomes a means for reassuring ourselves that we are truly okay. In a spiritual sense, we need to know our toil down here is going to be worth God's attention and ultimate congratulations. For this reason, succeeding at something is essential as new creatures in Christ. To this end, we set out to prove we were worthy of divine recognition and the checkered flag.

4. Attachment. The need to feel as if we belong to someone is basic to our spiritual and psychological natures. Being social creatures, we need attachment to feel complete. So, our search begins for the person or thing with whom we may unite in order to feel spiritually whole. Discovering how to find our Divine Mentor is essential in this regard.

5. Reward. The need for tangible proof of our worth is part of our spiritual make-up. In this context, we view temporal rewards as a shadow of what our eternal destiny must hold. Such thoughts propel us into living out our lives in a very compulsive manner. Here the emphasis isn't just on proving ourselves worthy, but getting rich in the process. We need to know that our human spirit is getting a handle on life's object lessons. At the same time, we slip into believing that the size of our bank account (or length of our trophy shelf) tells us what our Maker must think of us. Collecting things or getting rich signifies something of our heavenly reward. Only then can we be certain our Creator is genuinely pleased with us.

In Revelation 1–3, Jesus has already told us what sort of eternal rewards we can look forward to when he returns: a crown of life, a heavenly home, a new name, a reward according to our deeds, authority over the nations, new white garments, a place as pillars in his holy temple, and "dinner" with Jesus. No comparison to rewards here on earth!

FACING A HARD CHOICE

The Samson Test helps us see what happens if we attempt to meet the needs of our inner man all by ourselves. The end result is a false self, a person who fools himself into believing that he doesn't need anything. The true self—the redeemed person we are becoming in Christ—offers a voice of opposition to this belief thanks to the Holy Spirit. This voice reminds us that we must acknowledge our primary need for the Lord if we are going to get anywhere in life. It also speaks of how all of our other needs must be met by means of a partnership with the living God.

Nearly two thousand years ago, the apostle Paul explained the reason for our mental debate between truth and falsehood. In Romans 8, he advised, "For you did not receive [at conversion] the spirit of bondage again to fear, but you received the Spirit of adoption by whom we cry out, 'Abba Father'" (Rom. 8:15). With our new birth in Christ, something mysterious happens. We gain the Holy Spirit, whose mission is to tell us we belong to God. God's Spirit replaces the spirit we are born with, the spirit of fear. Now, both sides of our nature, old and new, begin a debate that may be lifelong.

In Galatians Paul helps us hear the oratory of the opposing sides: "And because you are sons, God has sent forth the Spirit of His Son into your hearts, crying out, 'Abba Father!' Therefore you are no longer a slave but a son, and if a son, then an heir of God through Christ" (Gal. 4:6-7). Our new spirit in Christ wants us to call out to the Father as "Daddy-God" when we're afraid. Our old nature is just as happy reaching for the needle, the six-pack, or the racing sheet when life gets too hard. It prefers that we listen to our flesh and remain slaves.

GOING THE WAY OF THE CROSS

God's solution for this ongoing debate is to cut to the chase. He knows our many fears actually are intensified by our compulsions. We may feel better temporarily after having relied on some old habit once more, but we're no closer to a solution for our problems. In the absence of real solutions, life only becomes scarier for us. Consequently, the heavenly Father asks us to hand in some compulsion (usually one at a time) in order to be free of those things that silently hold us in bondage to fear.

Surrendering my many obsessions about my appearance was a cross I would be asked to bear. God wanted to show me what I had been trying to ignore: I was born a mortal, bound to be imperfect. My imperfections silently convinced me I was bound to be alone. After all, who else would want me? Yet nothing could have been further from the truth.

Whatever our personal crosses may be, they represent for us what the cross represented for Jesus himself: an opportunity to relinquish the human will for something better—God's will. We are asked to lay down a part of our lives in a spirit of willing release to the Father. Past the grave of uncertainty, old habits get surrendered to the Lord for something new. We discover life after death.

The Bible calls this *sanctification.* The whole sanctifying process is a lifelong attempt by the Lord to teach us how to hope in him. He's got something better waiting for us beyond that gulf of fear or the conviction that our newest gimmick is bound to make us feel better. He's got a spiritual life in Christ that becomes a source of lasting reward. All we have to do is yield to God's purposes for our lives.

Being *sanctified* means to be "set apart." God sets down the rules and we learn how to comply, thereby separating ourselves from a dark and dying world with an eye toward all those gimmicks yet to be invented. As we surrender to the idea that there is life beyond our many fears, our choices and our lifestyles begin to change. Pleasing the Father becomes very important to us. In fact, we take on a whole new identity that bears witness to our new name and spirit as Christians.

Sanctification occurs by way of the cross. It involves hardship and suffering through the loss of familiar things. This promotes the death of the human will and makes eternal life begin in the here and now. The apostle Peter told us as much: "Therefore, since Christ suffered for us in the flesh, arm yourselves also with the same mind, for he who has suffered in the flesh has ceased from sin, that he no longer should live the rest of his time in the flesh for the lusts of men, but for the will of God" (1 Pet. 4:1-2). Suffering the losses of those things we have held dear becomes God's way of getting us to let go of our own agendas. His agenda takes precedence because it's the only one left to hold on to. Meanwhile, fears over our mortality fall away.

LOSING TO GAIN

I remember being at a local dive one night in order to have a good time. I was trying to get my mind off the toil of my workday, while preparing for a little hard-earned fun. I didn't belong in the place, but that didn't matter. I was out for a good time. Besides, I now was hiding under a newly purchased hairpiece. I wanted to see what my friends' reaction would be.

Old friends had crept back into my life since my conversion. Even though they all knew I was a "Jesus freak" now, they liked flaunting temptation in front of me. I usually obliged by joining them whenever they called. My self-serving heart said I still had the right to a little fun since being spiritual seemed less than rewarding.

On this particular night, the seating arrangements put me next to a woman at the bar. She was no one special, but she was there to drink like everyone else. That made her a comrade in arms. Our revelry was in full swing, even though somewhere inside my slumbering conscience I knew it was all wrong. Yet I figured God wouldn't mind if I didn't make too much noise. At least, that way my poor witness hopefully would go unnoticed. I was obviously rationalizing my heart's true intent to side with evil for a few hours.

The moment somebody started assaulting the Cross, I was doomed. A couple of seats down, one of my buddies was in a friendly disagreement with the man sitting next to him. My friend was insisting that the guy buy the next round for everybody and this fellow was quite naturally saying, "No way!" My friend had, in jest, begun chanting, "Crucify him, crucify him," and everybody was joining in. I halfheartedly did too, not liking what I was doing (or saying) but not wanting to be seen as a snob. The blasphemous chant didn't catch anybody's ear, except the Lord's. And I probably was the only one in the place whose spirit knew better.

In that same moment, I inadvertently knocked over my mug of beer right into the lap of the woman beside me. In a show of hilarity and good sportsmanship, she returned the favor by reaching over and grabbing for my head. She probably intended to ruffle my hair, but she loosened the moorings of my "rug" instead. Aghast, she and I both watched as my new hairpiece flew to the floor. In his mercy, the Lord showed me what "letting my hair down" would ultimately mean for me—his likely departure.

I left the bar shortly after my scalping. I felt horribly demoralized, but I quickly saw the implications. I had to surrender the right to go the way of the world when things didn't work out. More to the point, I had to lose my hair (just like Samson) to gain the look God was after. Hair had provided a pseudo image of strength and perfection for me, which in turn allowed me to deny a lack of genuine substance. I was quickly becoming a shallow person (even as a Christian), who was perfectly satisfied with the habitual.

THE WAY BEYOND THE GRAVE

Samson's story will show all of us that the loss of pride and personal possessions brings us to a place of rest in God the Father, while the Spirit of his Son begins to fill the emptiness inside. Jesus wants to show us how to die (like Samson) so that we might finally live. After all, unless the seeds of our old habits and desires fall to the ground and expire, we can't become spiritually whole (see John 12:24). Nor will we ever be free of the suspicion that our compulsions may be our only consolation in this life.

We must discover that the acceptance, fulfillment, success, reward, and attachment we long for are truly available to us by living in agreement with God's itinerary. His plan involves our exchanging the temporal things of this world for something eternal, so that our spirits can become acquainted with his way of running things. We accomplish this by looking to Jesus as an example of how to survive the death of our wills.

Jesus showed us how to let go of the human agenda. He marked out the path for conceding to God's will for our lives. He did this by going to the Garden of Gethsemane on the last night of his earthly life. There, he prayed and fought with his flesh, sweating great drops of blood on our behalf. He struggled to put aside any inclination to find another plan for paying the debt for our sin. He knew he had a job to do and proceeded to the cross to accomplish it (see Luke 22:39-46).

Because Jesus went the route of Gethsemane, the Bible tells us that Jesus can empathize with our struggles. He experienced human frailty and fear at its worst (Heb. 4:14-16). Therefore, his Spirit can assist us in our own struggles. Jesus' very real presence can strengthen us in our choice to serve God through divine conscription.

OUR GETHSEMANE EXPERIENCE

In this sense, a garden experience similar to Jesus' awaits all of us. It is the only means for drawing nearer to the Carpenter from Galilee and becoming like-minded in our hearts. It is also the only way into the arms of the Father who wishes to comfort us as we die to self. To find Jesus in that dark moment, we must follow a well-worn path with signposts that read:

- Expect the dying to self to feel awful and to take time.

- See the path of surrender as a beginning and not the end of your life. Remind yourself that there is life after death through the resurrection power of the Holy Spirit. This is because the pain of loss points us toward the proven character God promises as an outcome.

- Tell yourself that being afraid is okay for now. God will give you the strength you need to get through this season in your life. He promises you the victory you seek through his grace.

- Remind yourself that dying is time-limited. God won't let you suffer too long. Remember that life after death represents God's promise to never take anything away without replacing it with something better.

THINGS TO THINK ABOUT AND DO

Following are some how-tos for going through a Gethsemane experience of your own. Find a garden of your own to pray in—a quiet place where you can bare your heart to the Lord.

1. Confess your compulsions. Now, in faith, tell the Lord you're willing to give up trying to keep these things. If you need help, ask the Lord to make you want to give them up. Write them down and nail the list to a piece of wood; symbolically release those desires to the power of the cross and Christ's shed blood. Then find a group to join, so that dying to these things is made a little easier through the support of others.

2. Begin thinking about the things you don't like about yourself and the ways you've been trying to alter them. Write them out, so you won't forget what they are. Ask yourself how you would be different if you had to accept these awful things. Look for ways God might actually use them to strengthen you, and write down your thoughts and feelings.

3. Be honest with the Lord and yourself by admitting that your will is getting in the way and that you're resisting God's plan for your life. Now, drink the cup of bitterness. This means swallowing your pride. Allow the tears to flow or the anger to surface, knowing that self-will carries many emotions. Write a letter to God, telling him how this feels.

5

LIES ABOUT GOD

How can we ever get beyond fear, if we can't get beyond our own silly misperceptions about who God is? This was a question that was answered for me by an inmate I once worked with. He told me a fascinating story about how the Lord had changed his life by fostering a more accurate portrayal of the heavenly Father's heart.

This man had been a downright nasty guy who made a vocation out of robbing people. Holding people up was something he took great pride in; violence was mostly done for fun, ensuring his place at the top of his dark world. However, he was aware of the emptiness of his soul and decided to attend a meeting of the Promise Keepers, a Christian men's movement, at the Los Angeles Colosseum. There he gave his heart to the Lord. From that moment on his life was different.

He told me he had always believed in a God who was harsh and ready to judge him. He had learned all about this kind of God from his grandpa, who raised him. He told me his grandfather would beat him with a belt and tell him that the Lord was going to send him "straight to hell" if he didn't straighten up. Now, with his new birth in Christ, the man suddenly realized he had never known the truth about the Lord. The speakers he heard at the Promise Keepers event told him about a heavenly Father willing to forgive him for everything he had ever done wrong in his life.

After his conversion, my new brother in the Lord felt convicted to turn himself in. Now, mind you, he could have simply given up his "trade" and become a law-abiding citizen without the police ever knowing who he was. Nevertheless, he felt certain he was supposed to give himself up—knowing that doing so would probably lead to time in the state penitentiary. He walked the twelve miles between his apartment and the local police station to do what he knew the Lord wanted him to do. The one thing that kept him going was an overwhelming feeling that God loved him.

At the police station, the desk sergeant didn't quite believe what he was hearing. Criminals usually don't turn themselves in, yet here was one ready to tell his whole story. When he finally confessed to one of the strictest municipal judges around, the judge said he felt moved to show kindness to someone who was so obviously ready to live his life differently. He granted one of the most lenient sentences ever handed down for a man with such a long list of crimes.

This young man never would have discovered the Lord's favor had he not decided to trust a new image of God. The apostle Paul pointed out that our old way of seeing things keeps us stuck in the Samson trap. We need to be taught how to put off the "old self," which is basically corrupt. The process involves a change of mental attitude (see Eph. 4:20-24). Paul knew that our attitudes about a lot of things are dead wrong, yet they prevent us from getting to the end of our story successfully.

One of the things we fail to understand about God's character is that we can't size him up or pigeonhole him in our thinking. The Old Testament patriarch Job once said that God is so big, he can't be placed in any kind of conceptual container. God, he mused, "does great things past finding out, yes, wonders without number. If He goes by me, I do not see Him; if He moves past, I do not perceive Him; if He takes away, who can hinder Him? Who can say to Him, 'What are You doing?'" (Job 9:10-12).

Our need to size up the Lord is built on the suspicion that he is unreachable. His holiness makes him that way. So we give God an identity that makes him seem familiar. We attribute qualities to the Lord based on people and events from our past. Sad to say, a kind of wrongful intuition takes the place of an earnest search of Scripture to find out who God truly is.

MANOAH'S REVELATION

We have no way of knowing what effect Manoah's past might have had on his relationship with the Lord. Yet, some interesting idiosyncracies in his personality come to the surface in his attempts to get a handle on God in relation to his own son's life. The Lord needed to approach Manoah in a rather obtuse fashion in bringing further revelation of Samson's impending birth.

We read that the angel again visited Manoah's wife (not Manoah) after he prayed to the Lord to reveal additional insights about his son's arrival (Judg. 13:8). Bible scholars Kenneth Barker and John R. Kohlenberger suggest in the *Zondervan Bible Commentary on the Old Testament* that Manoah was understandably nervous about raising such an unusual child. But they go on to say that when the angel finally conceded to talk to Manoah face to face, "The angel did not directly answer Manoah's questions," implying that "his request for a confirming visit showed a lack of faith." They speculate that Manoah "was not convinced by the word of God."

Manoah offered the angel a meal and entered into casual conversation by asking the angel his name. It seems he was trying to disarm this holy messenger in hope of getting the angel to provide the inside "scoop" on things (see Judg. 13:15-18). It is obvious that all of these negotiating tactics were a measure of Manoah's mistrust of the Lord. Why?

For most of us, the person we become in such circumstances is a by-product of who we have had to be in our relationships with our earthly guardians—whether father, mother, or others who ruled over us. In this context, we may give up on the Lord because we view him as unapproachable or presume that God will always be hidden from view. Our distorted image of him bears witness to a perception we have of people who have stood in authority over us. Understandably, any fear they helped create will cause our initial impressions of God to be at least slightly sinister. Hence, learning to relate to him as our Father in heaven may be very difficult.

Our emotional bloodlines reflect the fact that we have survived parental upbringing through the power of buttering-up, conniving, or simply learning how to avoid them. We presume that in order to get anywhere with the heavenly Father we will have to resort to the same old tricks. Worse yet, these tricks will often be imperceptible to us. They simply will be a part of how we see the world and the way we normally react to people (or situations) who unconsciously remind us of the distant memories and authorities in our lives.

In truth, our requests of the Lord hinge on what we assume we must do to please this false image inside. The good news about our Abba Father, however, is something that takes a lifetime to get used to: he "is able to do exceedingly abundantly above all that we ask or think, according to the power that works in us." Because of that, Paul wrote, "To him be glory in the church by Christ Jesus throughout all ages, world without end. Amen" (Eph. 3:20-21).

EYES THAT SEE THE TRUTH

Manoah found out who the Lord truly was by being introduced to his mysterious nature. God's angelic envoy refused to be taken in by Manoah's flattery. The angel insisted on setting the rules for their brief encounter. Furthermore, the angel's identity (along with the Lord's) would ultimately be revealed by something more substantial than mere conjecture. Jehovah wished to remind all of us that he is truly trustworthy. He is described as a God of miracles, signs, and wonders, and he is willing to back up his claim (see Acts 5:12).

Once Manoah had been instructed in how to make a suitable sacrifice to the Lord, God's ministering spirit gloriously ascended to heaven. Manoah was forced to see the faulty God-image inside his heart that needed to be pushed aside. God wasn't someone who was going to be outsmarted (or out-talked) anytime soon.

What had stood in the way of Manoah's heartfelt appreciation of God's character was something called *transference*. This term represents what we do with the feelings we have toward the most important people from our past, if those feelings go unresolved—we transfer them onto other individuals. Manoah was no different from many of us. We earthbound types will often call upon the name of the Lord without seeing who we are truly relating to inwardly. The image of those who raised us lies deep within our spirit and colors our perception of God, but we don't recognize that fact.

Transference issues hinder us in appreciating Jehovah's character and the name that goes with it. His name is the one offered to Moses on Mount Sinai by God himself. The Lord told Moses that his name was "I AM WHO I AM" (Exod. 3:14). Simply put, God is who he wants to be. When we approach him, we must keep this fact in mind. In order to get past the many lies inside our heads about God's presumed nature, our expectations of the Father must begin to conform to a single profound truth—God's name means "I Can Do It All."

CELESTIAL PERFORMANCE ANXIETY

"John" was a new Christian whom I met at a Bible study. I had been a Christian for a while, but John still reminded me of me. He seemed to be sure he was responsible for motivating himself toward excellence. His only challenge was determining what to strive for next in becoming all that God wanted him to be.

It was apparent he hated anything about himself that constituted a spiritual shortcoming. John was always telling the group what he had done wrong the preceding week in trying to be the kind of Christian he thought he was supposed to be. He agonized over silly things like "breaking down" and buying a pack of cigarettes—after promising the group he had finally given up smoking, because God wanted him to. Everyone could tell that John saw the Lord as a very critical parent. His despairing spirit even had me convinced that God must be disappointed with me, too. I needlessly began keeping a tight check on my spirit. Much time was spent in self-indignation and prayer while I squirmed with the notion that something worse than baldness might happen next, if God couldn't be pacified.

A pervasive fear of rejection and feelings of insecurity were robbing John of his Christian joy. This happens when we don't know who God really is. A kind of celestial performance anxiety sets in, by which we attempt to please the Father whose real character remains a mystery.

I have heard testimonies from people who said that the Lord gave them the very thing they had been seeking all their lives only after some long ordeal. Their stories invariably had happy endings, but I assumed such endings were God's way of telling a person he had developed the attitude he was after. All one had to do was outlast God's scrutiny and strive for the character reform he apparently was seeking. If a happy ending proved elusive, well, that simply meant God wasn't satisfied yet. You just had to try all the harder.

All of this mental torture is predicated on the presumption that we can analyze God. If we know what he wants, then we have the luxury of getting ourselves to heaven, as well as the door holding our prize. There are many advantages to this arrangement. For one thing, having to wait for somebody when we're in a hurry can slow things up. For another, figuring the Lord out helps keep us one step ahead of his critical eye and any need he might have to tell us we have done things all wrong.

FEAR IS A LIAR

John was forcing God to be only as big as his fearful nature would allow. In John's case, this happened to be very small. The Lord's greatest gift to any of us is the opportunity to be free of our fretful natures and any need to put the "squeeze" on him. The surest way the heavenly Father has of accomplishing this monumental task is for him to get to the roots of our fears about being little in the company of someone big. Such fears clearly make our hearts obsess over all kinds of things.

Getting to the bottom of things in our hearts provides us with the valuable insight that fear is a liar. It is based on erroneous perceptions and judgments about how things are in this world. Discovering those lies helps us see the truth of how we view ourselves and God. Then, our many wrong beliefs can be corrected.

The Lord accomplishes this goal in part by directing us to his Word, where the truth about his character can be studied and taken to heart (see John 17:17). It is the only means we have of gaining the freedom from fear that we long for; it sets our thinking straight about who God is (Rom. 12:2).

The apostle Paul told believers what God's other method may be for correcting our vision of things: "For our light affliction, which is but for a moment, is working for us a far more exceeding and eternal weight of glory; while we do not look at the things which are seen, but at the things which are not seen. For the things which are seen are temporary, but the things which are not seen are eternal" (2 Cor. 4:17-18). Paul reminds us once more that our frustrations are permitted for our own good. They can help us see our many misperceptions about who God is.

In talking to John about his preoccupation with sin, I discovered a man holding onto several lies about God. He was seething inside because his hopes and dreams of becoming a lawyer had vanished. He had failed to pass the bar exam eight times and had finally given up trying. Meanwhile, he told me that his father was an attorney and had always assumed he would become one also. As a kid, he and his father had planned what college he would go to (Dad's alma mater, of course) and how the two of them would ultimately share a thriving law practice. John talked about the fact that once he had become a Christian, he hoped the Lord might help him realize his dreams of being a lawyer, "just like Dad."

John alluded to feeling as if he didn't count for anything with God. He was angry about the Lord's unwillingness to protect him from his own sense of failure. His anger at God was quickly denied, however. John reasoned that the Lord was simply waiting for him to get his act together before he blessed him. John scrambled to minimize his emotional losses while trying to figure out what God must secretly want from him. The problem was that he had a multitude of ill feelings about God as a Father. Pleasing him was going to be impossible.

AN UNHEAVENLY TRANSFERENCE

When John heard I was counselor, he quickly became a bundle of information. He wanted me to hear everything about his past, and I listened. John saw the Lord as someone very familiar to him. He perceived that God ran the universe in much the same way his father had run things at home. His dad brought home a paycheck, fixed things around the house on occasion, but was seldom seen because his law practice required long hours at the office. All of his father's hard work as an attorney meant there wasn't much time for John. Still, John always felt he needed to respect his dad. He simply learned how to hide his disappointment over his dad never wanting to play catch with him—or do a hundred other things.

I suggested that he was undoubtedly projecting a lot of feelings from his upbringing onto his image of his heavenly Father. I tried to explain the mechanisms of something called negative transference to John, and he hung on every word. He realized that God had become the object of his own transference issues.

Actually, God's invisible presence makes it easy to project many feelings his way. He becomes a kind of empty blackboard upon which we can scrawl any number of thoughts about his character. We also project a lot of feelings onto him because he comes saying he wants to be our spiritual Dad. What a set-up for anybody brave enough to try to love us when we're still smarting over what we didn't get from our original fathers. Thus, the Lord becomes the object of an unheavenly and highly negative transference.

Caretaker issues abound for us as men. Our dads or moms (or whoever played the part of grown-up) have assumed a crucial role in our becoming the men we are. Their shadows haunt our lives. We either had to follow their example or try to avoid it in order to turn out all right as men. Transference issues tell us that anyone who casts a similar shadow must be watched carefully.

The unresolved issues from our childhoods get in the way of our establishing a sense of closeness to our heavenly Father in the here and now. We will project highly charged feelings that will make a lasting faith in him hard to come by. Worst of all, our view of things will foster a lingering sense of abandonment in our spiritual lives. We'll feel alone because our perception of God will convince us he can't be trusted. And if God cannot be trusted, where else can we possibly turn?

Obviously, all the lies about God's character etched on our un- consciousness must be recognized. Only then can we replace them with the truth. In this way, we come to know the Father, someone vastly different from any human being we have ever met.

OUT IN THE OPEN

To bring truth to our relationship with him, the Lord first works to expose our wrong feelings for what they are—emotions having nothing to do with the Lord but which stand in the way of our spiritual well being.

God's exposure of John's transference issues began one Saturday when he and I were putting up a shelving unit in his garage. The project had taken all day, but John and I were proud of what we accomplished together. We had firsthand evidence that we were still men: we could build things!

John spent the entire time referring to himself as a "spiritual orphan." He said God didn't seem to respond to any of his prayers about things that mattered most. John sensed he simply was not a part of God's household. I knew underneath all of these feelings was a little boy who had been ignored by a father too busy to notice a needy child wanting to spend time with him.

Things had not been much different for me. My father's drinking problem had left me feeling alone and afraid. I spent a lot of time murmuring to myself and God about how alone I felt once I became a Christian. These feelings were accentuated after my father com-

mitted suicide in the early days of my Christianity. A sense of abandonment was never far away after that.

John and I were equally unhappy campers, but I was letting John
do all the talking. I was too cowardly to be vocal. Yet, underneath
it all I felt like God had ditched me too. We were about to discover
that the Lord wanted our bad moods out in the open. Murmuring
would get us nowhere.

Finally, John looked up at me and asked the really big question:
"What good is God's grace anyway?" He screamed out the question
a second time, looking up at the garage ceiling. In the same instant
John voiced his displeasure with the Lord, the entire shelving unit
came crashing to the floor. The bolts gave way, and down it came.
Hours of hard labor and self-absorption had all been for naught.
Our masterpiece lay in a heap at John's feet.

For John, this moment would have eternal significance. His anger
finally got the best of him. I'm sure it came riding in on a wave
of revulsion at himself. He was ready to blame the Lord for not
letting him succeed at anything. Out poured the rage. Silently, mine
poured out too. John kicked the mass of lumber on the floor. John
even told the Lord he hated him, cursing and saying he wished he
had never met Jesus.

When the screaming stopped, we sheepishly looked at one another and reached out to give each other a bear hug. We also began
laughing uncontrollably. Suddenly, comfort washed over me as God
ministered to my heart. Now that our anger had been acknowledged,
our hearts could be penetrated with the truth. I knew that our heavenly Father had been there all along—right beside us—and I shared
this revelation with John. By now, he was starting to pick things
up, and he looked over at me and said, "I've never really trusted
the Lord. I've always felt I had to prove myself to him first. No
wonder I've been so mad at him."

Years later, I ran into John and learned he had finally passed
his bar exam. He was practicing with a Christian law firm and
was happier than he had ever been in his life. He was very grate-
ful that the Lord had shown him the way past his self-hatred and

the feelings of detachment he had always felt.

Every time I reflect on that experience at John's house. I realize an important truth. God's presence is the only thing that keeps our lives bolted together. John had asked the Lord, "What good is your grace?" God provided a definitive answer. He removed his spiritual bolts (otherwise called grace) there in John's garage, showing both of us how fragile our existence really is apart from him. Perhaps King David said it best when he wrote,

> Indeed, You have made my days as handbreadths, and my age is as nothing before You; certainly every man at his best state is but vapor. Surely every man walks about like a shadow; surely they busy themselves in vain; he heaps up riches, and does not know who will gather them. And now, Lord, what do I wait for? My hope is in You. (Ps. 39:5-7)

Our experience helped me feel at peace in my spirit knowing how big—and encompassing—God's grace is. I also started to understand the basics of my own personality.

FIXING OURSELVES

My own sour spirit had been a substitute for self-confidence. Anger and fear told me I could hide my mistakes and imperfections behind perfectionism and self-contempt. It was the only thing that motivated me to get ahead. I saw this more clearly as God brought images of my childhood into view. As a little boy, I remember recklessly breaking things. I would first try fixing them, even if they didn't need fixing, and then proceed to break them anyway. Breaking toys made me feel powerful.

My dad had been a master fixer of everything. He was equally methodical about how things were to be done. I had stood beside him many times wishing I could fix things, just like him. At times, I even asked him to let me try fixing the very thing he might be working on. And sometimes he would grant the request, but never for long. I was just a little boy creating a bother. So, he would take over once more and I would silently slip away, thinking I had done it all wrong. I would never get to be like my father. Worse yet, I would always be denied the feeling of success (at anything) that would permit me to get beyond the fear that enveloped my soul.

What a tender trap my dad's perfectionism was for me. Feelings of abandonment were the by-product of my father's workaholic nature. As the Lord showed me my past from the perspective of my childish need to get my father's attention, I saw prison bars of shame forming in front of me. Those bars encompassed the Samson trap. I had placed my hopes for masculine redemption in the wrong person—me.

I began to see that an underlying rage had defaced my scalp forever. I had wanted to break what I couldn't fix. It was my scorn toward myself that prompted me to seek safety in madness. The doctors who were given permission to alter me repeatedly were instruments of my own contempt for an impoverished sense of self. James Masterson speculated on the same thing in his book *The Search for the Real Self:* "It is the nature of the false self [our old nature] to save us from knowing the truth about our real selves, from penetrating the deeper causes of our unhappiness, from seeing ourselves as we really are—vulnerable, afraid, terrified, and unable to let our real selves emerge." From my point of view, this is only possible through God, who holds the blueprint for our new nature.

HAVING SPIRITUAL SURGERY

God wants to help us get past the shame inside our souls. We must face our shame if our silly way of seeing things is going to be corrected. God accomplishes this by exposing our warehouse of ill feelings about our earthly parents. Then he cuts away the lies that have helped our misperceptions run so deep.

The Lord has in mind something called *circumcision,* circumsion of the heart. Paul talks about it in his letter to the Romans (see Rom. 2:25-29). Circumcision involves the removal of those lies surrounding our hearts. The procedure is spiritual surgery, and it begins when the Lord permits our worlds to fall apart. When we see our fragile lives starting to come unbolted, we are stopped dead in our tracks and forced to look at the Lord as a true Father figure. In the process, we discover what we're really feeling toward him. Only then can God's Spirit move with the precision needed.

Spiritual circumcision of the heart takes a lifetime, but right thinking can speed the surgical process. We Samsons have to get it through our flabby hearts that when something goes wrong, it doesn't mean God is out to get us. Neither does it mean that we've done something wrong. We have to stop personalizing our frustrations and stop blaming ourselves for our imperfections. In addition, we need to be honest with God about our hurt and anger with him.

To begin, we need to ask ourselves what false impressions about God come with failure, then replace them with the truth. Lies are emotionally based in our past, while truth is based on God's Word. Consider the following list of lies I have contended with in my Christian walk. Each is followed by a biblical truth of who God really is.

Lies	Truth
God loses his patience	His mercy is everlasting (Ps. 106:1).
God expects more of me	He pities those who fear him (Ps. 103:13).
God keeps score	He doesn't deal with us according to our sins (Ps. 103:10).
God has favorites	He promises to have compassion on all of his children (Mic. 7:18).
God lets bad things happen	His kindness leads us through trials (Rom. 2:4).

Once we exchange the lies about God's character with the truth, our spiritual blockade is broken down. Next, we need to voice our bitterness over what our earthly parents/caretakers failed to do.

I learned I could do this through prayer. I figured the Lord knew all about the disdain inside and was inviting me to see it too. My anger was no surprise to him. Instead, he knew that I needed to redirect it toward a rightful image of its originator. Oftentimes, this was my father. Typically, I would recall a time when Dad let me down or hurt me through indifference. Then, I would tell the Lord how angry I was. I might even open my eyes during the prayer and direct my feelings toward an empty chair—imagining my father sitting there. I could yell or even pound on a cushion, if that seemed necessary. My desire was to be free of the anger inside. I trusted God to sanctify the whole process.

Out of this season of my life came a faith free of transference issues with the Lord and free of underlying shame. Shame is defeated when we learn to accept human imperfection. Shame over our shortcomings goes along with being a member of the human race. It tells us we're inadequate and can't do things right. That's why we need God.

CLIMBING PAST OUR SHAME

The Lord has led me through the following steps to climb past my shame and the transference issues it created for me. They may help you see where you are heading in your own walk with him.

- I had to recognize my anger and talk it out—not act it out. Acting out anger keeps us stuck with the misperception that nobody cares. It is a self-fulfilling means of keeping everyone at a safe distance. Dealing with our anger honestly forces us to confront the real pain underneath.

- I had to learn what it meant to go to the Father in faith, while facing my transference issues with him. I had to sort out what feelings belonged to my earthly father, so I could have a right relationship with the Lord.

- I had to let go of any expectations as to what God should do to make things better. My plan involved presuming things about God and trying to negotiate. His plan involved me lying down in the face of failure, while waiting for the surgery to begin. Seeing our worlds come apart, only to be glued back together, has much to teach us about who God really is.

■ I had to face up to my shame. Confiding in someone else about the pain inside helps us whittle our shame down to size. Silence only magnifies it.

THINGS TO THINK ABOUT AND DO

1. Are you uncertain if you're angry about anything? Take the "Mad Test." You're angry if you do the following with any regularity:

–complain a good deal	–don't listen (ever)
–disagree with everyone	–talk all the time
–spend lots of money	–deny being mad
–control everything	–never have enough
–never want to give in	–don't ask for anything
–sleep all the time	–fantasize all the time
–overeat (or drink)	–wish you were someone else
–avoid conflict (always)	–wish you could disappear
–never want to answer	–wish others would disappear
–always have the answer	–break your toys

Recognizing that you're angry is important, but so is learning how to express your anger in a healthy manner. I lead anger management groups and have discovered these suggestions helpful: Pound on a pillow or on your bed with both fists. Use a tennis racket or plastic baseball bat and hit a cushion on the floor in front of you. Scream into a pillow or in your car when you're driving somewhere. Throw some eggs into a bathtub. Hit a punching bag or life-sized inflatable mannequin.

If you have problems controlling your anger, choose some

nonaggressive ways of expressing it. As an example, you might learn to breathe deeply and count to ten before saying or doing anything. After cooling off a little, think about what made you angry and then write it out. If that doesn't work, go exercise first.

2. List all the ways you feel that God the Father is just like your dad or mom. List those fears that are aroused when you ask the Lord for something. How do you suppose he really feels about you? If you are afraid or feel suspicious of him, write a letter to God about how you perceive him.

3. Initiate a time of Bible study on God's character. We must be willing to see what the Father has revealed about himself in order to know what he's truly like.

6

GETTING PAST OUR NATURAL DESIRES

Faith, as we have seen, involves getting past fear and reaching a place of lasting hope in our hearts. We may fear being left behind or never being able to prove ourselves. We may fear being hurt by others or suffer from feeling like we will never belong. Winning at the game of Life can be truly exhausting. So much can go wrong on the way to Millionaire Estates.

Samson certainly grew up with a game board full of problems. However, there is a mysterious gap in the Bible's commentary between the time of his birth announcement and his arrival at manhood. We know nothing of his childhood and adolescence except "the child grew, and the Lord blessed him. And the Spirit of the Lord began to move upon him at Mahaneh Dan between Zorah and Eshtoal" (Judg. 13:24-25).

Yet, we can infer from reading between the lines and observing his behavior, that he was a living example of someone who needed to prove himself constantly. Once he passed puberty, it seems he needed to show off his prowess in outlandish ways. Sorry to say, he didn't convince anyone that he really was an adult. More often than not, he simply proved he was still a little boy who never learned to control his masculine urges.

It also seems Samson got everything he wanted as a child. His pseudo-adult demeanor suggests that his parents may have acquiesced to his every wish. In childhood, a tantrum was probably only a breath away if he heard the word *no*. And since nobody wants to put up with a screaming kid, little Sammy soon saw the world as his oyster.

CARNALITY IN A NUTSHELL

While screaming for that ice-cream cone might have gotten his parents to give in to him as a youngster, his demands later in life became more difficult to overlook.

Samson was controlled by the lust of his eyes and the lure of the Samson trap rather than the Holy Spirit. In modern terms, he was a carnal Christian. Carnality involves being led by our own wayward thoughts rather than by Christ's Spirit. Danger arises, because God always honors the exercise of our free wills. He is committed to letting us go the way of darkness, if that's what our hearts truly seek (Rom. 1). The good news is, he will always put up a fight for us first.

The Samson trap first manifested itself when Samson was drawn to the heathen women of the Philistines. Worse yet, Samson refused to listen to his father's attempts to talk him out of doing what God opposed. "Then his father and mother said to him, 'Is there no woman among the daughters of your brethren, or among all my people, that you must go and get a wife from the uncircumcised Philistines?' And Samson said to his father, 'Get her for me, for she pleases me well'" (Judg. 14:3).

The Greek philosopher Aristotle once mused, "I count him braver who overcomes his desires than him who conquers his enemies; for the hardest victory is victory over self." This was a victory that escaped Samson. He could not overcome his own libido. Selfishness dominated his childish heart.

WICKEDNESS IN HEAVENLY PLACES

The apostle Paul reminded all believers of a frightening reality concerning giving in to such impulses: "For we do not wrestle against flesh and blood, but against principalities, against powers, against the rulers of the darkness of this age, against spiritual hosts of wickedness in the heavenly places" (Eph. 6:12). Behind the urge to sin is the hierarchy of evil that seeks to take advantage of our moral lapses. In fact, when we have a go at something sinful, we very often are inviting Satan and his fellow demons to wrestle with us.

The dominion of darkness Paul described is governed by the devil and his angels. Scripture tells us that Satan was an angel who became willful and proud and challenged God for his throne. Ultimately, his confederation was defeated and he and the portion of the heavenly army that sided with him were thrown out of heaven.

The point Paul was making is that those things that twist our emotional arms in times of temptation are sometimes invisible to us and exist in heavenly places. As in Samson's case, we may be absolutely convinced about what will make us happy. But we won't necessarily be alone at the time of this profound insight. Some little voice inside our heads may be telling us that "boys just want to have fun"; it may be an agent of darkness doing the talking. Despite Hollywood's portrayal of demons, demonic influence over us is subtle, encouraging us to quietly and little by little bend our spirits to Satan's many lies.

In addition to these demonic influences, all of us are stuck with a mindset and urges arising out of something the Bible describes as the *old man*—and he isn't our earthly father. The "old man" is our original sin nature in the raw, which always wants to do things contrary to God. This natural state of corruption is contrasted in Scripture to the *new man,* who is born of the Holy Spirit. The "new man" is given the capacity to conduct himself in a way that pleases the Lord because his thoughts reflect God's thoughts.

The bad news is that our old nature doesn't go away upon conversion. It simply moves over for God's Spirit. Much like an obnoxious relative in the back seat of your car, it continues to chortle away over how we ought to be driving and what direction we should be going. It is impossible to satisfy, and it constantly haggles with

our new nature. Simply put, our sin nature isn't so certain it wants
to give up its home to the new nature. Cohabitation is what it has
in mind, and it can be pretty pushy about the whole thing. All the
while, demons stay safely out of sight, hoping to use our sin nature
to influence us.

We must remember that Satan is a scam artist and he will use
any tactic he can to undermine God's influence. His advantage in-
itially is that we are accustomed to giving into the flesh. Even after
we have sworn our allegiance to the Lord, the old nature continues
to tug on our hearts. Predictably, Satan's advice to us (silently whispered to our spirits) is to go the way of the flesh; it clearly beats
having to work at a life of purity.

As typifies the old nature, our carnal eyes see something attractive and we think we have to have it. Or our flesh gets itchy over
some deeply held desire, and we begin plotting. Or our prideful
spirit says we deserve the very best life has to offer, and the wheels
start turning.

All of this has to do with the fact that we remain hidden, relationally speaking. Feelings frighten us. Consequently, we cut ourselves off from one another and stand alone with our pain. Pain,
all the while, demands we do whatever we must to feel okay again.
Sin offers a handy remedy. I believe this is what Jesus was getting
at when he warned that if a house remains empty, demons may take
up residence there (Luke 11:24-26). Being emotional "loners"
means we're likely to be listening to the enemy's lies without thinking twice about it. We must see that our relational handicaps make
us prime company for the demons who want to be our best friends.

THE TIP OF A DEADLY ICEBERG

This feature of the Samson trap is like an iceberg. Nine-tenths of
it is below the surface.

This was certainly true for a friend of mine, "Bill," whom I had
known since childhood. He had become a Christian long before me
and was excited to hear that I finally had given my heart to the

Lord. He often called to see how I was doing as a young convert. Usually he got around to telling me how he was doing as well— which wasn't so hot.

Growing up, Bill had gotten whatever he wanted. I remember being jealous of him when birthdays rolled around, because he received everything imaginable. Yet, I also remember being in his house and watching his parents fight all the time. Invariably, their battles were about sex or money. Whenever his dad started yelling at his mom about "not getting any," Bill would quietly go to her side, as though trying to protect her.

Typically, then, Bill's mother would request money on behalf of "little Billy." Although he endlessly argued with his wife about spending too much, Bill's dad was always ready to offer him whatever cash was necessary to make his trip to the toy store a happy occasion. Spoiling Bill became his mother's vendetta against his father.

His parents made Bill's home dysfunctional and highly toxic. Their antagonism toward each other set Bill up as a pawn. He was constantly reminded by his father that his mom was "frigid" and Bill's mom insisted that her husband was "oversexed." Neither of Bill's parents could afford to lose this battle of wits, so he became a potential ally for their respective causes. Bill's toy collection grew by leaps and bounds.

THE WORLD, THE FLESH, AND THE DEVIL

Bill grew up spoiled, and becoming a Christian did little to alter his expectations. Every phone call included a description of his newest toy—a large screen TV, CD player, skis, or the latest BMW. He also shared that his marriage was falling apart, and he didn't get much out of going to church anymore. No wonder his new secretary at work caught his interest. Leaving his wife became his solution for a mid-life crisis that was mostly about being unhappy with himself.

It can be helpful to take a closer look at how Bill got suckered by the enemy in all of this. Satan introduced Bill to the idea of something extramarital through a video he saw long before he ever met his new secretary. It had been soft-core porn produced under the banner of a legitimate Hollywood studio. The plot involved the hero cheating on his wife and having the time of his life. At the time, Bill told me about the movie and even recommended that I give it a try. Obviously, this fantasy thrilled Bill for reasons he couldn't explain. He later told me he couldn't get it off his mind after he saw it the first time. For weeks, he obsessed over that movie and always felt compelled to rent it one more time from the local video store—but only when his wife was away. The sex scenes were intoxicating.

Bill had never learned to cope in his marriage. He simply bought his wife whatever she wanted. He never figured out how to give her his heart. What needed to happen was for Bill to see how wounded he was on the inside and how that wounding made sin all the more appealing. Bill's relational difficulties were magnified by that part of his sin nature that remained unrepentant. In the midst of the relational vacuum that characterized his marriage, Bill found himself drawn to all that the devil had to offer. Bill had been educated on how to survive relationships as a child; sex and possessions were meant to keep everybody happy in an unhappy home. However, Bill never learned how to relate to a woman effectively.

We are probably not accustomed to seeing our sin natures in the context of not knowing how to relate to others as adults. Well, we must recognize that the old man is a composite of old behaviors, thoughts, and desires built on the premise that our pain is solely our problem. (Hiding from our inadequacies is a must. And that, in turn, makes Satan's work so much easier.)

SATAN'S LOFTY LOGIC

Given our propensity for staying hidden, Satan's ploys may be seen as cunning indeed. His dialogue with us is carried out in such a way that the "truth" about how we can secure happiness seems quintessential. It smacks of reasoning at its best, and we can't argue with the logic. Our spirits aren't strong enough to offer a rebuttal. More importantly, our loneliness demands a relational Band-Aid—and Satan insists his solutions are "ouchless."

When the Spirit of God comes into our lives, he tells us the truth. Unfortunately, these new truths lack any sense of that familiar logic to which we've grown accustomed. After all, the world has been our classroom. In practical terms, we are deafened to the lies. God's truth is foreign and doesn't satisfy the flesh's need for more of the familiar.

When the Holy Spirit arrives on the scene, he faces a situation similar to the one faced by King Hezekiah in ancient times. Hezekiah assumed the throne after a long line of rulers who had chased idols and forgotten the Lord. Proper worship in the magnificent temple in Jerusalem—the one built by Solomon—had ceased, and the temple itself had fallen into horrible disrepair.

When he assumed the role of Judah's reigning monarch, Hezekiah's first act was to gather the priests of the land for an important announcement. He demanded a form of worship that was truly holy. To the Levites, who were responsible for fulfilling the priestly duties in the temple, he said, "Hear me, Levites! Now sanctify yourselves, sanctify the house of the Lord God of your fathers, and carry out the rubbish from the holy place" (2 Chron. 29:5).

The new king also told them that the by-product of the nation's sin was the loss of freedom due to foreign armies advancing into their country. As he pointed out, "For indeed, because of this, our fathers have fallen by the sword; and our sons, our daughters, and our wives are in captivity" (2 Chron. 29:9). When we allow sin to rule us, we and our loved ones may become captives to our own deceit, emotional destitution, and financial ruin. Worse yet, demonic activity can be encouraged through our ignorance.

THE COST OF OUR IGNORANCE

One evening after work, I decided to do what I did most nights as a baby Christian home alone: I smoked marijuana. It filled the empty hours and helped ease my feelings of anger and shame I felt as a hairless man. Besides, there was nothing horribly evil about this practice as far as I was concerned. But what did I know? I didn't realize there were unseen forces waiting to join me in my quiet reverie. God did, and out of kindness he decided to lift the veil of my childish ignorance. He needed to show me what was ready to infiltrate my mind.

After I had a few hits and was getting comfortable in my favorite easy chair, something frightening transpired. A dark presence suddenly materialized. I began to shake uncontrollably. I felt as if I were going to die. I couldn't breathe, and I started perspiring heavily.

As soon as I began to pray, the apparition disappeared. I knew in that same instance that something sinister had been revealed to my conscious mind, so I wouldn't play with this brand of evil anymore. In God's mercy, I had been allowed to glimpse the dark enemy that opposed me. I learned my lesson well. I never smoked marijuana again.

The heavenly Father promises to give us a higher education than the one we have received from the world. By way of the Holy Spirit, we gain much-needed wisdom about the things that want to wrestle with us. In lifting the veil of our ignorance, the Spirit of Jesus prepares us to do battle with the forces of darkness that oppose us—with minds that are full of light, rather than empty and waiting for occupancy.

TAKING OUT THE GARBAGE

When we realize that our hearts have grown dusty and unworshipful, we need to clear them out. In essence, we need to rid our minds of the accumulated "rubbish," just as Hezekiah needed to remove the garbage from Israel's temple if God's people were to worship again.

From my point of view, removing the trash of the world's influence on our thinking demands something more of us than simply chasing down evil thoughts and trying our best to stop thinking them. We need a willingness to look inside toward our emotional shortcomings. We must see how our woundedness has enabled Satan to take us captive in our minds and hearts.

Through our unspoken grief or anger, our hearts have become silent, empty, isolated. And so our minds have sought any comfort we could find. Without our knowing it, demons have been around when we hurt the most, only too ready to offer a solution for our pain. But their prescriptions undoubtedly have brought us into bondage to false ideas. Serving their lies means we are yielding to their dominion over us.

HIDDEN TRAUMA

For Bill, there was a long season of painful discovery of how much he had missed out on as a child and adult. He had never felt loved as a little boy and had never known how to return love as a husband. He discovered this only after his second marriage—to his secretary—ended. At that point, he entered Christian counseling in order to address some of his issues.

He finally became able to admit that he had been suffering with a specific compulsive behavior that had plagued him since adolescence: masturbation. His emotionally barren household had been the enemy's classroom on loneliness and despair. Regretfully, he had learned that sexual appeasement was necessary for him to have any sense of belonging, the result of being introduced to pornography at an early age by his father. Dad had simply wanted to show Bill something his mother could never offer—a glance into manhood. Dad's pride won the next round with his wife, but Bill became the real loser. In adolescence, masturbation and scintillating pictures offered Bill a cure to an already damaged self-concept. Bill's counselor was able to help him see that he had grown up afraid of being close to anyone.

Now, as he told me his story over the phone, I could hear that fear. Bill had been afraid that his parents would divorce. He had been afraid of girls in high school because he didn't know how to relate to them. He had been afraid he would fail as a husband, and he had—twice. He had feared he would never be satisfied with life "as is" because he had never felt fulfilled, even as a Christian. Now, he was learning to cry with his counselor over all of this.

OUR UNSEEN ENEMY

Bill's wounds were deep, and the behaviors he used to cover up his imperfections were habitual. If the Holy Spirit hadn't helped him see the pain inside, he always would have been driven toward a compulsive form of adult sexuality. And it is likely another woman would have become his plaything.

Bill's counselor was able to help Bill see that settling for all those adult toys (including pornography) had allowed him to remain in hiding from his many fears. They simply meant he could appease his appetite for relationship a little longer. Beyond this, his counselor also helped him see that darkness had been granted an unfair advantage in his struggle for intimacy. This was because his compulsive need to return to things familiar, sexually speaking, resulted in his returning to the company of demonic spiritual beings and the logic they had to offer.

Over coffee one evening, Bill told me he had finally recognized how he was many times lured into watching something on TV on nights that he was determined to go to bed with his wife. Without knowing why, he would often feel compelled to turn on his television to a particular channel where he'd suddenly see a torrid love scene. The need to masturbate was just as suddenly awakened in him and his wife was left to go to bed alone. The "author" of this situation had become readily apparent to Bill. His fight to stop masturbating had consistently met with failure, as though someone was there to slip the wool over his eyes. Bill finally understood that it had been Satan all along.

Satan lost his advantage when Bill began to see how his fear of intimacy and the need to stay up late both arose out of feelings he had had about life at home with his parents. As long as those feelings went unannounced and unfelt, Bill remained relationally crippled.

He had been incapable of letting either of his wives know who he was because he had never learned how to be real with anyone.

In his counseling, Bill's tears and anger became routine—and for good reason. He had hungered for his parents' love but felt he hadn't deserved anything more than the cash they slipped his way. He had settled for a lie. Now, letting his heart express the truth of what it originally wanted meant the lie was losing its power over him. Thus, Bill's inner man found release through a godly relationship with his counselor, who afforded him the opportunity to show his pain.

FINDING THE "NEW CREATION"

To find the pain, we must look inward; the wound is inside our souls. Then it needs to be proclaimed and its pain released to the Father. Sadly, we Samsons prefer not to look inward, backward, or in any other direction; we are skilled at not taking stock of our lives at all. We shut our eyes to our problems and blindly choose to hold onto sin because it makes us feel better—at least temporarily. Once we decide to hide from the wounds of our past, Satan is handed a huge victory. We unwittingly invite spirits of darkness into our lives to help us fill the relational gaps. Subsequently, we fall into chronic patterns of sin as the enemy begins to oppress us.

Removing the advantage Satan has over us involves looking inward to the conditions of our souls and backward toward the events of our past. Ultimately, it also means looking upward to God's holy remedy, so our woundedness can be resolved once and for all. God's gracious response is to make us new creatures: "Therefore, if anyone is in Christ, he is a new creation; old things have passed away; behold, all things have become new" (2 Cor. 5:17). This new person is capable of being honest while speaking the truth of his heart. For this very reason, he is called a new creation, and his personhood becomes God's latest building project.

As we have already noted, built into the human spirit is a need to feel acceptable, fulfilled, successful, attached, and rewarded for

our efforts. These qualities represent qualities of our inner man subsequent to our new birth and drive us toward finding out who we
are and why we are here. God uses these needs to help steer us in
the direction of his throne room, as they become the driving force
behind our letting old things pass away.

By God's grand design, we begin to take on a holy awareness
of new things. The Holy Spirit breathes certain truths into our human spirit, helping us see that the sense of acceptance we hunger
for comes in pursuing godly character over an empty, store-bought
image. This is accomplished by making Jesus the Lord of our lives.
Finally, we feel acceptable to a special Someone. We also discover
that genuine fulfillment comes through experiencing lasting satisfaction (versus satiation) through God's Holy Spirit. Practically
speaking, this means letting God determine our lifestyle.

Meanwhile, we discover success in choosing heartfelt purity—
instead of power—as a way of getting ahead. Only then do we gain
the winning edge we seek. Next, we begin to understand that our
hunger for holy attachment can only be developed through a life
of discernment and increased sensitivity to God's invisible presence.
Cheap sentiment just won't do. Lastly, we realize our need for spiritual reward is established in learning how to appropriate God's grace
in lieu of the world's gratuities. This is the blueprint for the new
creation our heavenly Father asks us to endorse. It comes by way
of life in the Spirit and produces the inner man God has envisioned
since the Garden.

God's Word tell us that the Lord originally made us in his own
image (Gen. 1:27). Since his original model was ruined by sin, God
has to start over with us. His desire is to equip us with a spirit
strongly committed to serving him. He does this by allowing the
Spirit of his Son Jesus to live in our hearts. The faith that he supplies
through his grace becomes the means by which our personhood is
altered and we can finally throw the old man off the cliff.

For this reason, faith is the thumbprint of the Father on our souls.
It proves we are his holy property. As faith manifests itself in our
spiritual lives, it takes on distinct qualities that bear witness to God's

nature and supernatural habitation in our hearts. This is what the new creature inside our souls is all about. It is God's sandwich-board sign to the world, announcing that sin has not prevailed over creation after all. Being new creatures in terms of what drives us proves that we are God's finest piece of art. Through the presence of such things as godly character, purity of heart, and the like, we demonstrate a likeness to the Father and his Son Jesus.

The following table summarizes how we look at Point A in our search for the true self before our new birth and what counterfeits the old man in the flesh has probably settled for instead. It also reflects how we look if faith has prevailed over fear at Point B.

Point A: Old Man	Fear ← – – – – – – – – – – – – → Faith **Spiritual Needs**	Point B: New Man
Image	Acceptance	Character
Satiation	Fulfillment	Satisfaction
Power	Success	Purity
Sentiment	Attachment	Discernment
Gratuitousness	Reward	Grace

THE SAMSON TEST REVISITED

To come to terms with our spiritual journey toward God's vision of newness, let's take a look at your responses to the Samson Test presented in chapter 4. The test can be divided into five categories, or clusters, of personality traits. Each cluster consists of six questions to which you answered true or false. Each reflects an aspect of the old self, as measured by the presence of any counterfeit traits that have been erected to meet some spiritual need. It shows us whether faith or fear defines the inner man and to what degree the flesh remains unexchanged for life in the Spirit.

Fear and our sense of aloneness demand we come up with an alternative to the real thing, with falsehood being the best we can do. Thus, any one of the five fears identified through the Samson Test can be the motivation behind the counterfeit image we settle for.

CLUSTER 1: IMAGE, OR THE NEED FOR PUBLIC APPROVAL

Underlying Need	Predominant Fear	God's Remedy
Acceptance	Rejection	Character that Is Genuine

1. When I'm not looking my best, I'm "bugged."   T   F
2. When I goof up, I get down on myself.   T   F
3. When people disapprove of me, I get mad at them
   or myself.   T   F
4. When people approve of me, I don't necessarily believe
   what they're saying.   T   F
5. When I'm with a crowd, I feel I have to stand out in
   some way. Otherwise, I'll try to become invisible.   T   F
6. When somebody is watching, I get nervous about how
   I'm "doing."   T   F

CLUSTER 2: SATIATION, OR THE NEED TO BE FULL

Underlying Need	Predominant Fear	God's Remedy
Fulfillment	Purposelessness	Satisfaction in the Spirit

7. When I've given in to my favorite habit, I always feel
   like I need more.   T   F
8. When I'm having fun, I start thinking about what else
   I can do to have more fun.   T   F
9. When I want to have a good time, I need to be around
   people who can let down their hair and be slightly
   reckless.   T   F
10. When I want to let loose, I have to get a little "crazy."   T   F
11. When people don't see what I want from them, or my
    needs are not met right away, I get angry.   T   F
12. When I'm feeling edgy, doing something compulsive
    helps (for example, eating, drinking, having sex, or
    climbing Mt. Everest).   T   F

CLUSTER 3: POWER, OR THE NEED TO BE IN CONTROL

Underlying Need	Predominant Fear	God's Remedy
Success	Failure	Purity of Heart

13. When I've been put down or slighted, I feel hurt and think about getting even.   T   F
14. When I'm in control of things, I feel good.   T   F
15. When I don't know how to do something, I fake my way through without asking for help.   T   F
16. When I'm down, I think I'm just feeling sorry for myself.   T   F
17. When I play a game, I feel like I have to win.   T   F
18. When I feel like I'm not getting my point across, I end up yelling or breaking something.   T   F

CLUSTER 4: SENTIMENT, OR THE NEED FOR THE TANGIBLE AND/OR THE IMMEDIATE

Underlying Need	Predominant Fear	God's Remedy
Attachment	Isolation and Detachment	Discernment of the Invisible

19. When I'm alone, I get bored and resort to self-stimulation—pornography helps in this regard.   T   F
20. When someone says they care, I want proof.   T   F
21. When I'm tired, I usually turn on the TV and channel surf.   T   F
22. When I am feeling affectionate, getting physical seems essential.   T   F
23. When I try reading the Word, I end up daydreaming.   T   F
24. When people tell me I've disappointed them, I stop listening. I figure I just have to be me and they'll have to get used to it. Besides, life is too short to worry about all this.   T   F

CLUSTER 5: THE GRATUITOUS, OR THE NEED FOR EARTHLY TREASURE

Underlying Need	Predominant Fear	God's Remedy
Reward	Worthlessness	Grace that Is Sufficient

25. When I'm in a relationship, I invariably start thinking about what I have contributed versus what I have gotten in the deal. T F
26. When I feel like rewarding myself, something slightly extravagant usually fills the bill. T F
27. When I'm out with friends for dinner, I quickly figure out who paid the last time. T F
28. When I do something nice, I want people to say thank-you. T F
29. When I give up something, I think about what I might get in return. T F
30. When I get a gift, I usually think about other things I wanted more. T F

THINGS TO THINK ABOUT AND DO

1. Answering "True" to three or more items in any cluster means that this particular trait can be attributed to you. Score the results of the Samson Test and list the personality clusters that describe you. Try thinking of ways that each trait characterizes you, and write out your feelings about what the test has reflected about your personality.
2. Since this trait (or the others identified) is seen as a response to your fears, think about the things in your relational life that currently make you afraid. How do such fears manifest themselves and how do you compensate for them? Write out your impressions and ask a trusted friend or counselor for feedback concerning what you have written.
3. Try to recall a time when you believe Satan was trying to influ-

ence you in some way. How did his presence manifest itself, and what was your response? Write out your recollections. Also, think about how you might respond differently today, given your current level of spiritual maturity. Is that difference positive or negative? Why?

7

LONGING TO BELONG

A cceptance is the first spiritual need that characterizes our kind. Issues of acceptability are represented by anxious thoughts about God's true feelings toward us. Being human and subject to sin, we inwardly assume we will never be good enough to please the Lord. So we decide that rejection can be avoided by learning how to keep God happy anyway. As a result, "image" becomes our lifelong pursuit.

For most new believers, image is of utmost concern. We quickly see that God's faithful act a certain way, speak "Christianese," and belong to a unique culture to which we try to conform. Conformity helps us answer the really big question of what we must do to pass muster with the Lord. God's response to such tomfoolery is to show us that public image must be exchanged for godly character. We need to be men of substance who take on the likeness of Christ.

SAMSON'S TRAP AND GOD'S WILL

Samson was definitely into image. Self-absorption made his little heart tick. Picture him marching down to Timnah, contemplating the manly actions that would make his self-image certain (Judg. 14:1-3). He settled on sexual conquest. So what if Timnah was held by the enemy? So what if going there was against his parents' wishes? Any spiritual problems arising from such waywardness could be settled later—after Samson proved himself.

At the same time, God was planning to "move against the Philistines," and he believed Samson would do nicely as an instrument of his judgment (Judg. 14:4). God was intent on demonstrating his authority to the Philistines; he saw Samson's idiosyncracies as a place to begin. This typifies God's approach to the issue of who we are in Jesus. Our need to prove something to ourselves doesn't stop God from doing what he wants to do—which is to perfect us in Christ. Complexes don't prevent God's completion of us.

God's use of Samson began subtly. The Lord arranged for a lion to cross Samson's path en route to Timnah. While this deadly beast typified sin's intrusion in Samson's life, God used the event to demonstrate his ability to make sin's power inconsequential. Samson's reaction? "The Spirit of the Lord came mightily upon him, and he tore the lion apart as one would have torn apart a young goat, though he had nothing in his hand. But he did not tell his father or his mother what he had done" (Judg. 14:6). The Lord truly has rescued us from the dominion of darkness (see Col. 1:13). So, while Satan may want to do us in, the Holy Spirit is always ready to say, "Move over, son, and let me handle this." His help is certain.

Blinded by his preoccupation with self, Samson did not even offer a thank you for God's miraculous deliverance. Pride was undoubtedly taking its place beside pretense in Samson's attempt to hide from any sense of being ordinary. None of us Samson types can afford to give God the credit for the victories in our lives; we need the plaudits for ourselves.

RUNNING OUR OWN PROGRAM

Next, Scripture tells us that when Samson returned to get his newest fling,

> He turned aside to see the carcass of the lion. And behold, a swarm of bees and honey were in the carcass of the lion. He took some of it in his hands and went along, eating. When he

came to his father and mother, he gave some to them, and they also ate. But he did not tell them that he had taken the honey out of the carcass of the lion. (Judg. 14:8-9)

The Lord had warned the Jews through the Mosaic Law that touching anything dead would spiritually defile a person (Lev. 11:27). By typology, the heavenly Father was telling his people that sin and corruption were to be avoided at all cost. But Samson didn't pay attention. In his spiritual blindness, he lived outside the realm of consequence. He wanted to be able to serve the Lord without living by any of the Lord's rules. In short, he wanted to have his honey pot and eat it too. To further make his point, Samson went ahead and married the woman from Timnah. Self-absorption made his deluded thinking about all of this seem fairly routine.

Samson wrongly assumed that he could profess a faith in God but simultaneously "turn aside" to see the forbidden. He could even touch it if he wanted. According to his way of seeing things, it was his muscle—not God's power—that gained him the victory over adversity.

POINTING ALL THE FINGERS

In the early days of my Christianity, I met a fellow who strutted around as much as Samson. He too never realized how insecure he was and kept his eyes closed to prove it. I knew "Bob" from work and had a chance to sit down with him whenever our hospital staff got together to discuss a difficult case. I had come along as the newest member of the treatment team, and Bob—a social worker who had been on the same unit for years—made me feel immediately welcomed. I liked him because he seemed so self-confident. But Bob's insecurities slowly began to reveal themselves.

Everything Bob did seemed to be a countermeasure for feelings of inadequacy. Bob simply needed to show the world what a capable guy he was. For one thing, Bob's appearance was a point of fixation for him. Everyone could tell he spent countless hours worrying about his public image: his clothes were meticulous, his hair styled, and his nails neatly manicured.

He also spent lots of money proving what a fun guy he was. He insisted on picking up the tab whenever any of us would get together after work. His need for public recognition was obvious. He repeatedly volunteered to talk at the hospital's in-service meetings for staff, then he would conspicuously wait in the hallway for everyone to get around to saying, "What a great job, Bob!"

Sadly, image was all Bob had going for him. He knew nothing about trying to be a genuine human being—not even with his wife, the one person who should have counted the most. I could tell things weren't going well for them when I was invited to their house for dinner. Bob was bossy and critical. He complained about the way his wife prepared the meal and the fact that she had picked the wrong wine. He offered snide remarks about her appearance throughout the evening and made her the brunt of his many jokes.

Bob had decided to be miserable in his marriage, regardless of the fact that everyone else thought his wife was absolutely charming. The mirror of self-absorption he was standing in front of was telling him one thing: "My wife will never do." In truth, nobody would have been able to please Bob. Self-absorption guaranteed that he would always have the right to complain about things and point all the fingers.

MAKING THE GRADE

Bob was lacking a loving spirit for his wife because all he cared about was image. Godly character wasn't part of the picture. At the bottom of all this was his profound fear of never being acceptable to God, a wife, or anybody else.

Bob shared with me that he figured most people—including God—wanted only one thing from him: to do the job right. Otherwise, they might lose interest. Consequently, he had to prove he was the man to do everything. But whenever we got around to talking about what he personally wanted out of life, he couldn't say.

He surmised the need to excel was born from the fact that his parents had been professionals. They had taken him to a lot of seminars at which they were featured speakers, even though as a little boy he found these occasions extremely boring. Worse yet, he recalled how his parents insisted he wear a suit and tie to these functions. Grades had also been a point of concern with his parents. A's were the only thing acceptable to them.

When I asked him whether he ever felt loved by his parents, Bob looked at me quizzically and said he had never thought about it. He claimed that love had never seemed that important to him. Instead, getting his parents to be proud of him had become his life's goal. Even now, as an adult, he could admit that he often called them to tell them about something he had done at work, so they might be proud of his achievements. Sadly, however, their praise never came. He intimated that Mom or Dad would always tell him about some talk they had just given in some faraway place, and the conversation would invariably turn toward their most recent exploits.

SEEING OUR TRUE WORTH

Bob's fears over his personal well-being had turned on the question of whether he could prove himself to someone. His parents' childhood treatment of him had ensured that performance and image would be all that Bob would ultimately live for.

Only the Lord—not the critic inside our head—has the ability to show us our true worth. He wants us to see that the false image we have settled for is no longer necessary. The Lord did this for Bob in a miraculous way.

One morning, Bob sat glumly at his desk and told me he had just received some bad news from his doctor. Some tests he had recently undergone pointed toward a form of pancreatic cancer. He had apparently had this deadly disease for some time without knowing it. Now, Bob was told that his cancer was most likely inoperable; he had between six months and a year to live.

I had heard about how God sometimes healed people with the

laying on of hands. So, out of sheer desperation, I invited Bob to come to church with me one Sunday. That Sunday, a group of elders and myself gathered around Bob to pray and lay our hands on him. All of us hoped for the best, but I'm not sure any of us expected a real miracle.

At that moment, I was painfully aware that my own sin nature took precedence over everything else in my life. I was still a young Christian, and holiness seemed highly elusive. I had returned from a night of carousing just before dawn and sheepishly felt my carnal appetites would surely disqualify me from being any kind of "miracle worker." I had no illusions that God would want to answer my prayers for Bob. Meanwhile, during the prayer I began thinking about all those things Bob did to his wife that would probably disqualify him as well. I hoped that at least one of the elders in the group had a spiritual life strong enough to get God to listen.

Of course, none of this mattered to the Lord.

The next week, Bob went into the hospital for additional tests. When I went to visit him, he greeted me excitedly. He told me his doctors had just been in to see him with some news they couldn't explain. They told Bob that in poring over his x-rays and lab results, they had discovered the cancer was gone. They couldn't explain its strange disappearance, but remission appeared certain. In my heart of hearts, I knew for the first time that God was more powerful and gracious than I had ever imagined him to be.

There were still many questions left unanswered for me. How could the Lord have excused my darkened heart by responding to my prayer for Bob? Furthermore, how could the Lord have ignored the fact that Bob was a jerk? Both of us, in our own inimitable way, were nothing more than spiritual "Pig Pens." You know who I mean—the kid with all the dirt flying around him in the Peanuts comic strip. My assumption was that it must have been the other saints on the prayer team who were more saintly—that's what must have made the difference to God in his answering our collective prayer. Still, one question went unanswered for me: What did a person have to do to deserve a response from God?

The truth was that it served God's purpose to answer our prayer for Bob that Sunday. The Lord's response built all of us up in the faith. God proved himself faithful in an awesome way. Bob's miraculous recovery made his own sin nature suddenly appear defenseless against the Lord's incomprehensible might. It also accomplished something else. It helped me see I was eligible for his love just the way I was. Fears over a lack of acceptability began to disappear from that day on.

Bob must have discovered the same thing. When he returned to work, he was a different man. The image was gone. He seemed happy with himself, and he gave up the need to perform. He even became loving toward his wife. He told me that the idea of dying had changed his attitude about many things. For the first time in his life, he felt God truly cared about him. Like Ebenezer Scrooge, the ghost of his past could haunt him no more.

Knowing We're No Match

Image-making is meant to keep us in the spotlight. It is the only assurance we have that we're not going to be altogether forgotten. The Lord understands our hang-ups about such things and comes up with a perfect solution. He throws a lion in our path and quietly says, "Now, watch me." We can't beat that lion on our own and he knows it. With our ability to perform suddenly removed from the playing field, God gets to do his thing. We don't have to perform for him. Besides, it wouldn't do any good. All the applause we seek can't keep bad things from happening. God's character is the only thing that remains a certainty. Like Paul we will eventually be able to say,

> But what things were gain to me, these I have counted loss for Christ. But indeed I also count all things loss for the excellence of the knowledge of Christ Jesus my Lord, for whom I have suffered the loss of all things, and count them as rubbish, that I may gain Christ and be found in Him, not having

my own righteousness, which is from the law, but that which
is through faith in Christ, the righteousness which is from God
by faith. (Phil. 3:7-9)

The Lord makes sure we become new persons in Christ while experiencing the luxury of not having to rely on fakery any longer.
Instead, he shows us our sin nature can't stand in the way of his
having his way with us. We're going to make it to glory after all.
Over time, we even begin to see a mystery unfolding right before
our very eyes: we are taking on the likeness of our Savior. Thus,
any ugliness that might have prompted the world to turn up its nose
at us is mysteriously changed into something beautiful (2 Cor. 3:18).

THE IMPORTANCE OF DISCIPLESHIP

The primary means God has of accomplishing this change is
through a spiritual medium called discipleship. God doesn't really
want to have to put something as deadly as a lion in our path to
get us to see the truth of our dubious spirits. He knows we'd probably faint anyway. Instead, he does the same thing by putting dis-
ciplers in our path. They are meant to get us to see the erroneous
way we have of doing and seeing things. They are also given the
job of showing us God's Spirit, because they are issued the command to love us as God's ambassadors.

The first step is accomplished in our receiving the counsel of
someone who is, in effect, God's megaphone. In choosing to sit
under someone's spiritual authority, we make ourselves available to
their teaching. This is usually our pastor, to whom we lend our hearts
and minds in order to receive God's admonitions for our lives. A
vertical relationship with the Holy Spirit is fostered by applying the
truths revealed through our pastor's sermons and Bible study.

Next, we become partakers of a horizontal relationship with the
Holy Spirit by entering into fellowship with other believers. Here,
we turn our eyes and our hearts toward God through a support
system wherein everyone is made equal. Everyone benefits from

learning how to function as a singular body (1 Cor. 12:12).

Lastly, discipleship comes by way of a personal encounter with another believer with whom we make ourselves known heart to heart. Genuine relationship with another believer becomes a new source of learning about God's love and character, as well as who we are in Christ. Private interpretation of God's Word is finally made irrelevant

KEEPING OUR SINS A SECRET

"Stan" had only been married a year when he came to me for marriage counseling. He told me he felt ready to explode. His vexation was over wanting to live the life of a heterosexual while secretly desiring to act out homosexual impulses. In college he had experimented with one homosexual relationship and through his twenties had struggled with compulsive trips to gay bars.

But with marriage, a form of pseudospirituality had evolved in Stan's life. This meant going to church, getting up early to pray, and getting rid of his stash of pornographic magazines. Stan was convinced that this would keep God happy and his wife satisfied, that he was being the best Christian he knew how to be.

All the while, Stan was busy keeping his fantasy life a secret. He snuck home with adult videos whenever he could, his favorite theme being sexual liaisons between men. He reasoned that watching them on occasion was all right because he took them back the next day. At least they didn't sit in his closet like his magazines had. When I asked him if he had ever talked these things out with his wife, Stan was stunned. He figured he knew what being a Christian was supposed to look like, and he wasn't eager to be found out and destroy that image. Besides, he felt his fantasy life wasn't anybody else's business.

The problem was that Stan saw sin as something external to himself. He felt certain that it was primarily a spiritual issue with no lasting relational significance. That way, he could keep it strictly between God and himself. Stan made it a point to tell his wife what "respectable" sin he was currently working on whenever he wished to impress her. But he held the darkness inside his soul out of sight of his new bride.

WHEN BADNESS STANDS IN THE WAY

Stan had been a Christian a long time. However, he had never allowed God to speak to him in a personal way. In fact, he avoided God's presence by openly avoiding Scripture. He said that every time he scanned the Bible, he felt like he was getting a lecture. His solution was to quit reading it. For this reason, God's Word had never become living and relevant to him.

Stan avoided most church functions as well. He assumed his "badness" disqualified him from being a member of God's regular household. He knew he was saved, but assumed God the Father didn't want him hanging around other believers. Stan should have known better; he had received an undergraduate degree in biblical studies.

Now Stan could quote me the verses pertaining to the importance of confessing our sins to others (James 5:16). But he figured he got to choose which ones and how many. Consequently, Stan had never shared his sordid secret with another soul. Counseling was his first attempt at an intimate relationship with someone who could provide a mirror of truth as to who he was in Christ and how God felt about him.

Stan came to me because he felt my experience counseling homosexual men might be of some help to him. He allowed me to became a spokesperson for the Holy Spirit. This is what true discipleship is about—choosing to make ourselves vulnerable to the scrutiny of others in hope of discovering God's love for the broken person inside.

Stan said he had hoped to put sin away forever in asking "Connie" to be his wife. He recommitted his heart to the Lord just before asking her to marry him, figuring getting serious about the things of God would make the difference. A Christian marriage was going to magically guarantee his sincerity as a spiritual person. He assumed he wouldn't experience his former impulses and everything would be fine.

Good intentions mean nothing to someone who is avoiding the Spirit of Jesus out of fear. Change is contingent on God's mercy exclusively, not on man's efforts or best wishes (Rom. 9:16). Stan discovered this fact when his old lifestyle came to life once more. Being attracted to such things made Stan doubt the truth of his own heart. Maybe he had never truly asked Jesus into his heart. Or perhaps God had seen his depravity and turned away, deciding somebody else was more deserving of his love. Ultimately, these doubts compounded Stan's fears over his unacceptability and caused a slide toward darkness that became more extreme. Stan felt compelled to start finding male prostitutes on the side. Connie never suspected, and Stan's church attendance never faltered.

MISERY SEEKS COMPANY

It seems misery always seeks company and so does an evil heart. Just ask Samson. He got his parents to eat some of the forbidden honey. Stan tried to do the same with Connie. He wanted her to become a partner with him in his rationalization and compensation. He became more sexually demanding of her. His sin nature insisted that if she would simply excite him a little more, he might want to give up his need to act out homosexually. His urges were her fault.

If Stan had been honest with himself, he would have acknowledged that he wanted his wife to be a co-addict with him. He was simply trying to exchange one habit for another. Straight sex of a highly compulsive nature was going to liberate him from another less acceptable compulsion involving his sexuality. Stan demanded, pleaded, complained, and cajoled Connie into being the kind of person he thought he needed her to be sexually. Her happiness seemed less important than his being assured that his spiritual health could be proclaimed through straight sex. All the while, his desires for another gay experience were boiling inside.

Deep inside, Stan knew that things were going all wrong in his new marriage—mostly because of him. He and Connie were fighting, and they spent many nights feeling thoroughly defeated as to how to make their life together work.

I found out that Stan's erotic compulsions represented the only defense he had to protect himself from feelings of wretchedness. He had been sexually abused by an uncle when he was seven, and he had grown up feeling he was shamefully beyond help. Ironically, he had begun acting out the very thing he feared about himself—as typifies many victims. This is called *reenactment* and represents a person's need to repeat certain traumatic events in one's life in order to gain some sense of power and control over the feelings. True intimacy, meanwhile, seems out of the question.

HEARING AND RECEIVING THE TRUTH

God's solution was a simple one: Stan needed to learn how to hear and receive the truth about who he was in Christ—by way of my discipleship of his spirit. Through spiritual mentoring, Stan would learn of the true nature of his spiritual blindness and how it affected his relational and spiritual life.

Discipleship is based on a principle of accountability and a willingness to let someone else see our true character. We finally see ourselves honestly as the truth of God's love is made real to us. As we discover our heavenly Father is ready to love us—spiritual warts and all—we are equipped to give up being loners and image-mongers.

A relationship of this kind evolves as we look inward and recognize our fears. Other people scare us because they have the ability to hurt us. They may find out what's really wrong with us and leave us exposed. The Lord needs us to see that such fears are often fueled by misperceptions. We don't see people accurately because our wounds are linked with a child's way of seeing things.

Stan's childish mind suggested that denying his homosexual

urges was of paramount importance to his relational success. After all, they caused him to question his underlying masculinity. So he became demanding in the bedroom, confirming that he indeed was a "man" and had something of worth to offer the woman who had chosen him. The truth of his highly damaged sense of self-worth remained well protected, but fears of exposure and his wife's ultimate rejection were never far away.

God's first step in Stan's deliverance came when Connie stopped playing along. He came to one of our sessions frustrated that she had finally refused to give in to his incessant demands of her. She had emphatically said no one night and told him he had a real problem. At that point, he had begun hearing the truth.

I'm sure Connie learned to resist mostly to save her self-respect. But, due to the strength of her character, her actions forced Stan to admit that the problem was strictly his own. Getting his wife to be a co-addict simply wasn't working anyway. Through it all, Connie stuck by Stan and showed him that loving somebody involves not only saying "I do"; sometimes it means saying "I won't."

PATHWAY TO FREEDOM

The Lord used me to get Stan to talk about the little boy inside who was so afraid. I tried to consistently reflect the love of my heavenly Father to this man who revealed the depth of pain inside. Stan hated himself for how he had sought out his uncle's affection, even after he had been molested by him. I helped him see the loneliness of a little boy whose father left him and his mother through a sudden divorce. His need for a father's love had propelled Stan toward his uncle's attention. In the context of a dawning awareness of any child's appetite for affection, Stan could stop hating himself. At the same time, God's love was made uniquely available to his wounded heart.

Stan worked at sharing his past with me and saw how blind he was to the truth of his own pain. He wanted desperately to get to the hurt and anger within while giving his pained soul expression.

In truth, only the power of the Holy Spirit could soften Stan's heart. Sin had hardened it, which made honest disclosure and genuine repentance seem impossible. Yet, I told Stan that God would be faithful and supply him with the desire to give up his sin.

My attempts to be God's loving ear helped Stan get beyond his fear of exposure. Each time he told me he had given into his compulsion, I prayed for him and for the wounded child inside. Consequently, a sense of forgiveness was almost instantaneous. Slowly, the Holy Spirit began to melt his heart, and Stan discovered he was not reprehensible after all. This made the likelihood of true repentance even greater. Since he no longer needed to fear retribution, his heart softened into genuine sorrow for what had happened to him and what he was now doing to his wife.

LOVE MADE REAL

The Bible tells us that "the prayer of faith will save the sick, and the Lord will raise him up. And if he has committed sins, he will be forgiven. Confess your trespasses one to another, and pray for one another, that you may be healed. The effective, fervent prayer of a righteous man avails much" (James 5:15-16). Through the many prayers of a trusted counselor, Stan's soul was being healed.

My prayers of healing for Stan often involved waiting upon the Holy Spirit to show me a pattern of sin in Stan's life, then praying about the underlying wound. For instance, when hearing of Stan's need to hide in front of his TV every night, I realized his deep feeling of loneliness. His sense of not belonging became the focus of my prayers.

Hearing of Stan's uncertainty as to how the Lord must see him showed his fear of the Father. Therefore, I prayed that the Lord's love for Stan would be revealed. At the same time, I would have Stan sit in a chair, hold a pillow, and try to imagine being held by Jesus. It took some time, but Stan finally was able to feel safe with this level of spiritual intimacy—ultimately breaking down and crying.

The Prayer of Inner Healing

Such prayers of inner healing involve God's chosen disciple focusing on the underlying issues of the saint being ministered to, rather than the symptoms he lives with as a wounded individual. Such issues are somewhat hidden from view and often require exploring what happened in one's past. As an example, if a person faced separation and loss as a child, he will often live with chronic fears of abandonment. If someone saw violence, then he will unknowingly live with fears of death or destruction. The counselor who can read this situation will know how to pray for the issues of one's past in a fairly specific manner. This requires accurate discernment, along with a willingness to help the wounded saint look back in time toward the source of his ongoing discomfort.

Also, a genuine love relationship needs to be offered that reflects the mind and heart of Christ. This is the means by which believers are discipled. Being able to address the issues of our shameful past with someone who sincerely listens and cares about us makes God's own love tangible.

The fruit of this for Stan was a growing willingness to talk openly with his wife without fearing rejection. In addition, he was soon ready to join a local church support group geared toward helping homosexuals find a Christ-centered solution to their problem. God's Word came alive for Stan during this season. He began to read it daily and found it to be encouraging. It strengthened his sense of worth because he began to see how much the Lord loved him.

A Step in the Right Direction

Stan's erroneous perceptions about the nature of relationships kept him guarded and defensive. He felt the pressure was on him to perform sexually, avoiding catastrophe in his marriage and single-handedly refuting the belief that he was gay. Yet he couldn't possibly live up to his self-imposed expectations and, consequently, saw his character as suspect.

These misperceptions were born out of the abuse of his past. His conclusions about his uncle's actions were erroneous because a little boy simply isn't capable of understanding the pain of victimization. Instead, a child will tend to overestimate his own role, catastrophize what it all means, overgeneralize any fears related to its probable recurrence, filter out any positives about himself, and rely solely on emotions in dealing with the issues of victimization.

From this laundry list of cognitive information will arise a lifelong tendency to rely on the same set of beliefs to get by in the future. This is what we bring with us from a wounded childhood. For Stan, the tendency to overestimate his guilt and shame—and to expect the worst outcome—was extreme.

SEEING OUR BLIND SPOTS

Part of Stan's healing came when he began to see such distortions in his thinking about relationships. I began pointing out some of his misconceptions about how things *ought* to be in his relational world. These unstated beliefs made getting close to anyone impossible because they set him up to fail. Such misperceptions are fairly common for those of us who have learned to bank on image. They reflect the belief that we have to be extraordinary in some way in order to survive. Otherwise, we may try being very small, so no one notices.

More often than not, relational wounds from our past have made such beliefs a must in our minds. Being powerless in the past may have meant being hurt. Consequently, we decided long ago that being all powerful, all knowing, or generally invisible was the best antidote against a relapse of powerlessness.

Stan had to be taught how to think more rationally. I began by sharing some of the misperceptions experienced by those I've counseled professionally over the years.

- When something goes wrong, I always assume the worst. I magnify the negative and minimize the positive.

- I tend to overemphasize my importance in situations. For some reason, I don't feel free to be human and make mistakes.

- I project my feelings onto others. I figure I can read other people's minds.

- I tend to overidentify with things going on around me. I assume that if something has gone right (or wrong) it reflects on me.

- I think in very black-or-white terms. Things are either "just fine" or they are "just awful." Either I've done a good job or I've failed miserably.

- I believe Christians must never show a negative emotion.

These chronic patterns—and many more—are horribly self-defeating. In Stan's case, such thoughts kept him guarded and defensive. He couldn't possibly meet his self-imposed expectations. I showed Stan what a more balanced and rational opinion of himself would look like by having him write out some of the following responses. Each was a response to any distorted thought that might cross his mind pertaining to being acceptable:

- When things go wrong, I don't have to assume the worst. It just means I'm having a bad day and tomorrow will give me a chance to start over.

- I'm no better or worse than the next guy. Therefore, I just have to learn how to be me and accept the idea that I don't have to prove my righteousness, which is imparted to me by faith.

- Everything that happens to me doesn't necessarily carry a message from God. He's fair, but life isn't. Consequently, I will have to get used to life's unpredictability.

- My wife doesn't have to behave a certain way to keep my self-worth intact. My worth is kept safe in Christ.

- I don't have to assume that everything is about me. Some of my thoughts and feelings belong to my past, not my future. I am not deficient just because I thought or felt them.

PUBLIC IMAGE WON'T DO

If we venture a look at Samson once more, we may see the real problem he faced. It may be the case that Samson spent his whole life trying to live up to some terribly destructive misperceptions about being a Nazirite. He privately knew he didn't match up, but he undoubtedly felt he had to keep his deficiencies a secret.

From his point of view, he was supposed to be a holy man. His strength told him God still expected great things from him. Thus, he tried hard to establish a powerful public image in the absence of bona fide character. All the while, Samson practiced fooling everybody (including himself) into believing he could do it all.

Samson never reckoned with his sin nature, supposing he was perfect already. He never realized that his Nazirite code was meant to bring glory to God. It was intended as a promise from God—to always be with Samson in a special manner. He didn't have to worry about being perfect; he would always need the Lord to achieve his true potential.

God had wanted Samson to taste the fruits of spiritual victory over mediocrity and sin. He had given this man-child a look into the future by leaving him a lasting impression of what he could do in partnership with the Holy Spirit. That is what the episode with the lion was all about. God wanted a real relationship with his son. Samson simply needed to expose himself to God's presence and admit any weaknesses he had, so God could lead the way. That was the true source of lasting satisfaction.

THINGS TO THINK ABOUT AND DO

1. Most people who hurt inside think in a highly negative manner. In what sense do you continue to see things "the same old way" and how might such thoughts contribute to your sense of despair? Write down your impressions as to where these thoughts come from.

2. One way to change these patterns is to recognize negative thinking. Each time a negative thought arises, ask yourself, "Do I really want to think this way?" Quietly tell yourself, "No. This is a lie." Then try coming up with an alternative thought:

- "I don't have to have all the answers."

- "I don't want to generalize. Just because this situation arose once, I'm not going to think it will always happen this way or that it is all because of me."

- "I don't have to assume the worst. God says things will work out."

- "I don't have to keep score. It's simply not true that I always get cheated. I'm going to stop feeling sorry for myself."

8

WHEN FUN
DOESN'T SATISFY

For Samson types, the need to find personal fulfillment in life becomes more pronounced with age. No matter what follows, this thing we call "living" has to be accomplished in fewer years and to our lasting enjoyment. Only when we figure out how to make our seventy-plus years fun will our toil down here seem worth it.

In truth, we have settled for the idea that satiation is the answer. God insists that there is something more durable than the world's pleasures in gaining lasting satisfaction with life. His recommendation: discovering how to befriend Jesus.

THE ORIGINAL PARTY ANIMAL

Samson's fear about being cheated out of the good times can be seen during his wedding ceremony at Timnah (see Judg. 14:10-11). He was so sure that his one chance of sex with a centerfold would pass him by, he had the announcements in the mail before he even sprang the news on anyone. All the while, he was throwing caution to the wind: most of his invited guests were Philistines, who hated his guts.

Once the party was in full swing, Samson took the stage. Because he had to be the center of attention, he began telling riddles. We read: "Then Samson said to them, 'Let me pose a riddle to you. If you can correctly solve and explain it to me within the seven days of the feast, then I will give you thirty linen garments and thirty changes of clothing'" (Judg. 14:12). With a few drinks under his belt, Samson was the life of the party.

We must recognize how God wants to provide us with a deep sense of satisfaction in our souls by offering his love. His joy awaits us at no cost to our personal well-being. Yet our own ideas of "good times" keep him away. Too often we seek debauchery and satiation, figuring that putting Jesus on the guest list would mean a stern lecture and the end of our fun. So our plans usually involve looking for ways to "get away from it all" while hoping God isn't looking. Samson's escapism came by way of his need to be a prankster. It gave his superficial life meaning to be the joker in the crowd. The bad thing was that all of his jokes and riddles had a "gotcha" quality to them. He liked making people angry.

Predictably, the wedding guests tired of Samson's games. With nothing but contempt for him, the Philistine rabble warned his new wife that she had better sneak the answer to the riddle out of her husband or they would come back and torch the place (Judg. 14:15). Living life on the edge, as Samson did, usually comes at others' expense.

LIFE'S SCRIPT

Each of us lives out a script in life. Samson's script is probably obvious to any who have used drugs to get high: life is what we endure until the party begins.

Often, such a script is learned from our parents. Their way of handling problems teaches us a great deal about what we can expect from life and how we can get by in this world. These scripts usually are devoid of joy. After all, how can one find true happiness in the pursuit of those things which are strictly temporal? Money, booze, retirement—you name it. None of it is going to do the trick. Life still will seem empty after the buzz dissipates.

The only way we can find satisfaction that lasts is through discovering a deeper level of companionship with God's Holy Spirit.

The joy set before us involves seeing that the Lord wants to be our lifelong companion and best friend.

The apostle Peter put his finger on the real problem here. In his first epistle, he wrote that we are to "abstain from fleshly lusts which war against the soul" (1 Pet. 2:11). Simply put, we are at war with ourselves and Jesus' Spirit if we choose to go have fun without the Lord. The truly good times we crave can only be found through discovering God's idea of fun. Otherwise, satisfaction will be outside our grasp.

ARE WE HAVING FUN YET?

I met "Gene" through a mutual friend we'll call "Ted." The three of us got together on occasion to watch sports on TV and relive our glory days on the athletic field. All of us were armchair quarterbacks, "wannabe" jocks who had only fading memories to brag about. Our potbellies told us how things had turned out, but that didn't matter.

After spending some time together, I realized that Gene's idea of good times always involved doing things in excess or on the sly. Even though he was a Christian, R-rated movies were more naturally appealing to him than PG films. Violence, strong language, and a little skin helped keep his interest. Humor also had to be slightly raunchy for Gene. Dirty jokes always seemed funnier than straight jokes to him. Practical jokes were even better—if he got to be the joker.

The excess carried over to his play as well. Engaging in recreational activities meant Gene wanted to do twice as much in half the time. Every ounce of pleasure had to be wrung from the moment. For instance, he bragged about going on vacations with his family and doing more in three days than most people could do in a month. He bragged that spending eighteen-hour days behind the wheel on one of their treks was customary.

Whenever Gene got together with Ted and me, he was invariably the last guy who wanted to go home. Ten hours in front of the TV wasn't enough. He chided us for having to go home to our "old ladies." He felt it was his male duty to tell his wife his fun wasn't over until he said so—no matter how long he might be gone from the house.

Apparently, Gene was convinced that the good times were going to vanish sooner or later. Adulthood was only worth the effort if he could guarantee himself a good time.

How Are We Programmed?

Why do men go to such extremes? I believe it is the suspicion that life is bound to be cruel. Fear tells us that grabbing for the gusto is the only way to put off the inescapable disappointment. We don't really have any evidence to the contrary. Besides, we have been programmed to see life a certain way.

Gene, Ted, and I had the opportunity to go on a men-only weekend retreat with a group from our church. In one of our small group discussions, I heard Gene talk about his dad. In the process, I began to appreciate why he looked for fun times so desperately.

He shared that his father had been a reveler whose happiest moments were those spent in drinking and telling dirty jokes. He also apparently loved getting away from his wife and kids as much as possible. Ideally, nights away meant going to the local bar for an evening of adult pleasure with his male friends. That meant Gene didn't see his father much at night. When he did, his father was preoccupied with other things and unable to give him the attention he needed.

Gene was certain that money had been the "Kryptonite" that robbed his dad's spirit of its strength. He recalled how his father would look over his various checkbooks, obsessing about how much money had been saved that month. Not surprisingly, Gene's mom was scolded any time she went over budget buying food for the month.

All the money was being saved for his father's retirement because that was when his fun would truly begin. Gene's dad never got there, however. He had a sudden heart attack, and his savings went to his wife and the two kids. Gene was eleven years old when his father was found dead in the garage of their home. His father's sudden death had convinced Gene that life was mean and unpredictable.

Without realizing it, Gene was following in his father's footsteps. He had unknowingly taken on a script learned from watching his dad find his greatest enjoyment apart from the family. This script got acted out in Gene's mad dash for excitement. Underneath it all, Gene was angry at being abandoned by a father who searched for his own good times minus the wife and kids. When his heart ultimately failed him, Gene was left out in the cold for good.

RECOGNIZING FAMILY RULES

Our parental upbringing becomes a family script that gets repeated through the way we approach frustration as adults. It will very likely reflect the attitude our parents (or caretakers) left to us as an outlook on life.

Gene's father appeared down on life. He never acted happy about things and spent his time around the house blaming somebody else for this sorry state of affairs. Despair was his emotional birthright to Gene. On top of this, he left Gene alone to figure all of this out. Fear of never learning how to capture the carrot on the stick of life forced Gene into conceding to his father's shallow point of view. Seeing this fact helped Gene understand his own pursuit of happiness. Upon sharing this insight with the men who encircled him in our group, he began to miss his father all over again. Soon, tears flowed down his cheeks.

I had the chance to take the podium after our lunch break, and I talked about how disappointments with our parents carve out deep impressions in our hearts. We grow up convinced that our lives are inevitable, given what we have learned. And I suggested that we play by certain "rules." These rules are acquired unconsciously and represent the things we assume we must do to succeed, find meaning in life, or at least survive. Ultimately they evidence the unspoken ways our families dealt with things.

After listing some of these rules, I invited the men in attendance to come up with some of their own, depending on what they assumed their childhoods had taught them about survival. The following are the rules I identified during my talk and the conditions by which they most likely come into existence. Some of this material is taken from *The Anxiety and Phobia Workbook* by Edmund J. Bourne.

1. "One must strive for perfection, but never expect to succeed." This rule evolves from a life at home in which parents were overly critical. We are left with feelings of guilt and the belief that we'll never be good enough. Inferiority haunts us as we constantly work at things, but never attain satisfactory results.
2. "Things must be controlled or entirely possessed, otherwise they will be lost forever." This rule usually stems from significant losses in our childhood. Obviously, feelings of abandonment will prevail in a situation where divorce or the death of a loved one shows us that life means unpredictability and insecurity. Out of these experiences come overdependence on others and various addictions to fun, drugs, food, work, or whatever helps us hide from the pain inside.
3. "Getting close to someone is potentially harmful and must be avoided." This rule is the result of violence in our homes. Physical, sexual, or emotional abuse tells us that life is not only unfair, it's also dangerous. Feelings of inadequacy, mistrust, guilt, and rage combine to make us feel hostile toward life. We either give up and become self-made victims or turn around and victimize others. Either way, we let aggressive impulses live in our hearts that keep intimacy at bay.
4. "Feeling connected to anyone means looking outward—never inward—and striving to pretend that all is well, no matter how you feel." This rule is caused by dysfunction in our lives. Whatever the nature of that dysfunction, the craziness of our homes tells us that life is chaotic, unreliable, and generally unnerving.

To survive, we had to live out the family rules, where silence—denial of that craziness—and the ability to disregard one's own perceptions about things became our survival guide. From that environment, something called codependency was born. Now we live for the other guy because we personally don't count for anything.

5. "One should never strive to become attached." This rule is the result of parental rejection, overt or covert. Parents can too easily impart a feeling that a child was unwanted. Rejection convinces the child that his right to exist is questionable. We become self-made saboteurs who experience chronic failure on the job or in relationships.

6. "One is entitled and the world owes him something." This rule comes from parental overindulgence, or complete neglect of the child's need for the things of childhood (such as fun times, developmental milestones, or family traditions). The spoiled child is given insufficient exposure to deferred gratification or appropriate limits. Therefore, as adults we tend to be easily bored, lack persistence, or have difficulty getting started. On the other hand, if we have been given nothing, we assume that everything we've wanted is yet to come; we wait for the world to offer it to us on a silver tray. In either case, we want someone else to be responsible for our sense of well-being.

7. "Life is only safe as long as one never leaves the security of the immediate." This rule usually is the result of parental overprotection. The child who is overprotected never learns to trust the world outside of his immediate family. As adults, we may feel insecure in venturing away from home or out of view of the people to whom we've become attached. Uncertainty about tomorrow means we have to cling to what we have today and stop planning for the future. Striving to get ahead or be unique is pointless.

CHANGING YOUR OUTLOOK

The biblical account of the prodigal son highlights the importance of challenging such rules (see Luke 15). The father in the parable had two sons. Each presented a different outlook on life. The older son legally was entitled to the lion's share of the inheritance. Consequently, he figured the only way to be sure of his portion of the estate (and the rewards he deserved) was to stay close to the farm and please his father.

On the other hand, the younger son was a run-of-the-mill hedonist. He assumed the only way to get his reward was to get his portion of Dad's estate up front, and then go do what his wayward heart had always wanted—see Las Vegas (or at least its ancient equivalent). Each son mistrusted his father as a benefactor as well as what life held for him.

It took the younger son to set things right. After spending his wad, he came to his senses. Left with nothing, he began to realize how good he had it back home and quickly headed for the family farm, prepared to work as a servant. Rather than believing life was unfair, the prodigal decided to stop living according to some script. Instead, he changed his ways and went home. While the prodigal was still on the road home, his dad came running. He reached his son with open arms and gave him a big, wet kiss. Then, he decided to throw a party in honor of his boy who had been "lost," but now was "found" (Luke 15:24). Like the heavenly Father, Dad was overjoyed with his son's change of heart.

All the while, the older son just couldn't get into the swing of things. When the party was announced, all he could do was grunt and groan over the wasted money and how little his father appreciated all of his hard work. He reasoned his brother didn't deserve anything except a quick kick in the rear end.

THE THREE Rs

Sadly, we may be convinced (much like the prodigal and his brother) that life has to be approached in a certain way. We may believe that despair, bitterness, and scorn are justified emotions. We may take on lifestyles of fatalism, sarcasm, or some other "-ism," so that nothing takes us by surprise. Fear is typically behind it all, telling us to develop an attitude and hold on for dear life.

It was essential for the prodigal to recognize this unspoken belief in his heart. The familiarity of the fear that shrouded his thinking needed to be resisted, so that life could be lived out in a new way— free of self-fulfilling thoughts and ruminations. How did he accomplish this? I believe it involved a three-step process.

First, he had to resist the temptation to stay on in Vegas. Next, he had to return to his father's farm. Lastly, he had to learn how to receive his father's love. This process is the Holy Spirit's version of the "three Rs" we once learned in school. All of us must learn how to *resist, return,* and *receive,* in order to begin to live by the new rules the Holy Spirit is authoring for us.

1. Learning to Resist. Not giving in to the rules of our past means resisting the fearful thought that we'll never truly be happy. God's Word says that the Lord will fill us with joy when we stand in his presence. He wishes to give us eternal pleasures and a life of joy (see Ps. 16:11). This means we have to be close enough in spirit to reach for the things he wants to provide.

We draw closer to the Lord by obeying his Word and living according to his holy precepts. Old rules need to be exchanged for kingdom principles by which our happiness and peace of mind can be secured. The Bible is full of spiritual principles that are meant to show us how to live fruitful lives. They provide a guiding light through our dusty way of seeing things; they offer renewed hope that we can succeed on this earth. Here are some examples:

- The principle of reaping and sowing (see Gal. 6:7): what we put into something will determine how much joy we get out of the effort.

- The principle of giving (see Luke 6:38): generosity bears its own reward and provides God with an excuse for doing something nice for us.

■ The principle of forgiveness (see Matt. 6:14): God is ready to forgive us the moment we start forgiving others.

■ The principle of trusting God (see Ps. 32:10): Putting our faith in God results in his supplying us with his unfailing love.

■ The principle of waiting upon the Lord (see Is. 40:31): By letting God lead the way, we will be given renewed strength.

■ The principle of asking, seeking, and knocking (see Matt. 7:7-8): Pray about things, and we will find what we've been looking for.

Resisting ultimately means taking exception to anything contrary to God's will and calling it sin. What is required is a prayerful search of our hearts for the misguided rules that undoubtedly keep us heading in the wrong direction—toward either hedonism or legalism. In either case, we must be ready to repent of whatever we're doing that puts us at odds with the Father. If you're not certain, ask yourself what you do for fun that you'd be embarrassed to tell someone about at church. Avoiding it from now on seems essential for your well-being. Otherwise, ask yourself what kind of moral checklist you have been trying to get everybody else to live by. Then throw it away.

2. Making Our Return. In order to accomplish an about-face and return to the Father, we must face an old adversary. Satan stands in our path, wanting us to return to whatever script makes us feel better about things. He assumes that we Christians live in ignorance of who we are becoming in Christ. If he can make things go wrong in our lives, he knows we'll start feeling afraid again and think we are deficient. Our imaginations gladly do the enemy's dirty work. Jesus told us that Satan is a liar (John 8:44). Awful times don't mean God is mad or we're bad. Sometimes they mean the devil is up to his old tricks, trying to turn us back to Vegas.

Pushing the devil (or his lies) out of the way is essential for returning to the Father. This means standing up to fearful thoughts in the midst of hard times and rebuking their power over us. We can do this by identifying those thoughts telling us to mistrust the Father and acknowledging their falsehood. Listing them on paper and then refuting each one by finding an applicable Bible verse might prove helpful in this regard. Memorizing those verses then becomes our way of telling the enemy where to get off.

We must also acknowledge our favor before the Lord and proclaim that he is faithful, no matter how dark times may seem. Praying aloud may help, as we call on Jesus to help us overcome the power of circumstance to keep us prisoners to fear. Taking our list of fears and throwing it away—or putting a match to it—helps us see the power we have over darkness.

3. Learning to Receive. The final step may be the most difficult to learn: receiving requires figuring out how to be little again. To receive God's promises, we must learn to see ourselves as children while experiencing the joy of our salvation.

Our old nature doesn't want us relying on such silly notions. Living by the rules handed down to us seems to make more sense. Survival is hard enough without having to start over learning some new rule book.

This was certainly the case for my friend Ted. His sour look told everyone that being a Christian wasn't easy. He spent hours lecturing Gene and me on what being a spiritual leader was all about. He wanted us to see him as the spiritual head of his home. He let us know that if we hoped to accomplish the same thing, hard work was ahead for us. We would need to get up early to read God's Word. We also shouldn't pass up any "drive time" on the freeway; sermons on tape should be our first priority, followed by Christian talk shows and evangelical preachers who spoke on the half hour.

Fun times for Ted meant attending as many Christian seminars as he could, so he could be a better husband, father, or man on the job. If things suddenly went bad for Ted, he ran down his list of "shoulds." For example, financial problems meant his tithing record must be deficient. He overlooked the possibility that he was spending too much money on things he didn't need.

The weekend Ted, Gene, and I spent on the retreat was truly eye-opening for all of us. Ted discovered that his legalistic script for life had been learned at the hands of a father who was an ordained minister. Even though Dad had never pastored a church (becoming an insurance salesman instead), he had run his family as if it were his congregation. Meanwhile, arguments were never tolerated between Ted and his brothers. Dad simply stepped in and said each participant needed to go to his room and think how their actions were highly displeasing to the Lord. They could come out of their rooms only when they were ready to tell the entire family what sin they were ready to confess.

LIVING UNDER A CURSE

Feedback from the men in his small group helped Ted see how legalistic his approach to life had become. His fearful spirit told him that when things went wrong, something religious needed to be done about it. Now, through the encouragement of other men, Ted began to see the truth. God wanted him to approach his personal problems with a sense of freedom in Christ—to work things out, practically speaking. He needn't obsess over his performance as a saint.

Like Ted, we need to recognize that living by the rules—even if highly spiritual—brings some form of bad news. The devil is anxiously waiting for us to try legalism or hedonism as a way to settle the question of what life is really all about. He knows that choosing either takes us away from the care of the heavenly Father.

Paul wrote that anybody who attempts to get through life by observing the law places himself under a "curse" (Gal. 3:10). This is because legalism directs us toward the law of self-judgment, just as surely as hedonism leads us toward the law of self-reward. Either way, we hand ourselves over to the control of darkness in the process, much to Satan's glee.

GIVING UP THE RULE BOOK

Several weeks later, Ted announced that he had done something bold. He decided to give up religious practices for awhile. Daily Bible study was given up for an early morning run, so he could start the day feeling more energized. He then admitted he had even purchased a new CD for the car, the newest release of one of his favorite rock bands. All of these changes were predicated on the belief that God loved him as is; he didn't need to work nearly so hard at pleasing the Father. Nor did he have to figure out how to achieve righteousness. That was God's job.

As time went by, Ted conveyed that his attempts to give up his rule book were eye-opening. He had started hearing from the Lord almost immediately, and things at home started to improve dramatically. Remarkably, he said he had discovered that time with his wife could be entertaining. The two of them had recently spent several evenings together, playing games and enjoying each other's company. They had happened on this great idea mostly by accident, when Ted's wife found nothing but reruns on TV one night and he decided to not get lost in his newest Christian how-to book. Coincidence, along with a gentle nudge from the Holy Spirit, had pushed them in the direction of doing something fun with their evenings rather than avoid each other. Better yet, Ted and his wife had experienced a kind of second honeymoon together. Holding hands and taking walks at night became their treat to one another for the evening. Even their lovemaking had improved, according to Ted. All the while, fights about finances waned because Ted began to listen to his wife. She had always insisted that their budget could be modified, but he had usually wanted to pray about it first and her plan was never heard. Now, it was actually being implemented.

JESUS: OUR SOURCE OF HOPE

Ted's countenance changed through this season of his life. He no longer looked like somebody who had just eaten a lemon. He even said he felt like a kid again. The Holy Spirit had convinced him to give up needing to find the answers through religious scrutiny. Life's many questions could be approached with a childlike faith in the Lord. Things would work out because God was in charge and ready to come up with the solutions.

The Spirit of Jesus wants to show all of us that our source of hope in the Father comes down to learning how to be kids once more. He introduces us to the idea that God is a loving Father who isn't expecting anything more from us than a childlike trust that he has everything figured out. With this revolutionary idea in our hearts, the Lord's comfort can begin to change us from the frightened creatures we are to the exuberant children he wants us to be. Fear can be replaced with hope.

At the times of our greatest frustration, Jesus is ready to offer a special brand of hope through his presence. His Holy Spirit bears the name of Comforter, and he dwells in the heart of every believer. When despair or fear enters our spirits, we can choose to give up the old rule book and look for the Father's blessing through the Holy Spirit's words of encouragement.

Circumstances don't have to be frightening; they can be enlightening. Imagine sitting in a small boat in the middle of a big lake along with a bunch of guys from work. Maybe it's what you guys have spent the whole year dreaming about: a vacation to end all vacations—away from the wives—with a little fishing thrown in. And, best of all, Jesus has decided to come along because he knows the best spots on the lake.

After the first day is nearly over, though, no one has caught a single fish. Everybody is dog tired because you've been up since dawn. Everything will be fine, however, as soon as you get back to the cabin and put the Wheaties out for dinner. The problem is that you're stuck; a storm has blown in and the waves are making everyone a little seasick—everyone except Jesus. He is asleep in the front of the boat.

As the waves grow more menacing, the boat begins to take on water and everybody starts bailing. The lake suddenly looks as broad as the Atlantic Ocean. You begin to wonder how far you'd be able to swim if the boat goes down. Swimming has never been one of your favorite sports, and now you're remembering that all the life jackets are back on the dock. The idiot who forgot them should be thrown overboard, except you were the guy assigned the duty of stowing them on board. Meanwhile, you hear a sound you can't quite believe. Jesus is snoring. How can the guy be sleeping when everybody is about to die?

The disciples faced this predicament on one of their many excursions out on the Sea of Galilee (Matt. 8:23-27). A storm arose that put them in touch with the smallness of their souls in a threatening world. It became a prime opportunity for the Lord to turn circumstances around and transform perspiration into inspiration on behalf of his little ones. It's a situation many lost souls in this world can identify with: we're sinking, and God is fast asleep. But our spirits can soar. Jesus' Spirit is near with comfort and peace and the desire to demonstrate the Father's kindness to his offspring.

Upon awakening from his snooze, Jesus spoke a gentle rebuke to his disciples: "'Why are you fearful, O you of little faith?' Then He arose and rebuked the winds and the sea. And there was great calm" (Matt. 8:26). The Lord wants us to trust in him as our Savior. When the disciples finally stopped their frenzied activity of bailing, cursing, and struggling, they looked toward Jesus.

At that moment, there was great calm for them. Jesus could take his turn at doing something about the situation, and he wasn't going to fail his friends. Instead, he would bring the Father into focus. All the while, an important lesson in faith was being written on their hearts. If the Lord is sleeping up front, then all must be well. Otherwise, he'd be up, doing something about it.

GROWING DOWN

I know that worrying about things seems more satisfying than trusting in the Lord. But we should at least try to learn the steps that will help us to develop a childlike trust in Jesus' care.

In practical terms, this will involve going to God's Word when times are tough and expecting to be comforted by the Father. We should read until we have that hope and then hold on to it. Writing out a verse that breathes the truth of God's kindness to our spirit is also important. Reminding ourselves of that verse throughout the day will get us through the storms of life. Then, when bedtime comes, that verse can be the one we quote to ourselves before we close our eyes and go to sleep.

Learning how to "grow down" becomes essential. Growing down translates into practicing being little in the Lord's care. This means giving up the need to be busy as hedonists or legalists. Kids don't want to be busy, they want to enjoy themselves. Sadly, we adults forget how to do this. We're caught up in trying to figure out how to get a handle on life first. So, I have attempted to define the means for growing down as a measure of the Lord's commitment to save us from worry. Let us take a look at what it entails and start practicing these things today.

- Accept the fact that it's okay to fail. God isn't keeping score. Life's lessons aren't about getting it right—this time. Instead, those lessons are meant to teach us about how to accept God's grace in order to try again—as often as needed.

- Risk change—it's fun. Life doesn't have to be approached through a list of shoulds and shouldn'ts. It can be lived out as an invitation from the Holy Spirit to relax and find out who the Father truly is.

- Learn to be silly. Being silly means learning how to take life less seriously and enjoy it more.

- Learn to share with others. This means giving when there's enough to go around and realizing that God will supply everyone's needs when there isn't. You don't have to be a sacrificial lamb in this regard. If someone needs something you cannot give, stop feeling guilty and start praying that the Father meets his or her needs.

- Learn to obey God's Word in order to find lasting peace for your soul. It takes practice, and it's not a matter of doing it by the rules. Obedience comes in wanting to please a Father whose kindness will ultimately turn your wayward heart around. You'll just want to do what "Dad" asks of you because his love will be proven to you.

- Learn to say, "I'm sorry!" when you've hurt someone, even if the other person is wrong. God loves to see his kids being peacemakers.

- Accept the idea that going to Jesus when times are tough gives him the chance to be your ship's Captain. He loves to bring great calm when we face storms. If you feel like you're sinking, cry out to him and let him know you're afraid.

- Try approaching life one day at a time. Don't get ahead of the Lord as you travel the path of righteousness together. He knows the pace that is best for you.

- Learn to see life as a pop quiz instead of a final exam. God isn't grading your performance anyway. Besides, Jesus has already taken the test on your behalf and passed with flying colors.

THINGS TO THINK ABOUT AND DO

1. Make a list of the tacit rules you live by, and see if you can remember how they originated in your life.
2. Write down some of the things you may have seen your parents do that convinced you to live life in some rehearsed manner. Write a prayer to the Lord asking him to help you live by his kingdom principles.

3. Look over the items mentioned in the how-to's of growing down. Keep a daily journal of the ways you think you were able to be "little" in God's care. At the end of each day, list the things that got in the way of being little and pray about these things. Remember, God is at work in you.

9

Exchanging Power for Purity

Men are typically overachievers in some fashion, and our attempts to prove ourselves help determine our identities. Whether we apply our best efforts to becoming the company's new CEO or the street gang's most fearless member, winning seems essential in showing the world we are truly men.

In striving to get ahead, we often find cheating is to our advantage. Our old nature settles for the lie that worldly promotion can be gained through the power of trickery and the ability to fool the slob next to us. After all, we hate losing.

God's plan runs counter to such thinking. Scripture shows us that worldly power can be exchanged for purity of heart—and that's exactly what we need to get ahead in our spiritual and emotional lives. The path of domination simply leads to corruption. We may finish the race first, but nobody will be left in the grandstands to join us in the celebration because they won't be able to stomach our twisted morality.

The Lord wants us to learn how to achieve success without losing our friends along the way. He fosters purity of heart and helps us learn how to get ahead by getting behind everybody else. If this sounds like a riddle, you're right. God loves to give us brainteasers by which his truths are made more evident. They usually involve gaining a new, paradoxical way of seeing and doing things.

SAMSON'S RIDDLE

Samson loved to pose riddles, too. During his wedding at Timnah, his Philistine guests were given a real brainteaser and had seven days to come up with an answer. "So he said to them: 'Out of the eater came something to eat, and out of the strong came something sweet.' Now for three days they could not explain the riddle" (Judg. 14:14). Everybody at the party was determined to come up with an answer. No Philistine wanted some Hebrew to get the best of him. Male pride was on the line.

In bottom-line terms, we men realize that to amount to anything, we have to succeed at something. Success is proof that we count. Short of that, we fear we will be seen as nerds, goofballs, or the one member of the team made to ride the bench. Our fear of ending up the jerk who couldn't get it right is a strong motivator toward expedience.

Cheating is one method that appeals to our carnal instincts. It convinces us we really can prove ourselves—at least to the people we swindle along the way. Cheating on our taxes, our bosses, or on our wives becomes the only way of assuring ourselves we'll finally get the brass ring.

Samson was a cheat and so was his new bride. She knew how to get what she wanted, particularly when her life depended on it. For seven days, she played the part of "victim" with her husband. She cried and carried on so much he couldn't stand it. Her feigned melancholy was the result of her looking out for her own interests. She understood that by getting Samson to share the answer with her—which she would then pass along to her Philistine comrades—she would undoubtedly save face and, quite likely, her own skin (Judg. 14:16-17).

Samson couldn't resist. His wife's feminine wiles got the best of him, and he told her everything. She then shared the secret with her relatives. Predictably, Samson turned violent and decided to strike back. That often happens when swindlers get swindled.

Sadly, Samson never learned what honoring his wife meant, or what staying at home felt like. He had his male pride to think of. Once the party was over and the secret was out, he was off to the nearest Philistine outpost to vent his rage on the scoundrels who had gotten the best of him. He traveled south to Ashkelon and murdered thirty Philistines. To add insult to the massacre, he removed the clothes from the corpses of the recently departed Philistines and handed them out to his honored guests.

CHEATING IS IN OUR BLOOD

Survival of the smartest is simply an extension of the principle of the fittest outlasting everyone else. Cheating, lying, or thieving become means for getting by in a world that rewards the Samson in all of us.

How can his special brand of lawlessness be overcome? The answer comes in recognizing that cheating is in our blood. It is passing through our spiritual veins at this very moment. Scripture tells us that while God is true, everybody else is a liar (Rom. 3:4). Nobody can escape this mortal flaw in the human personality: the need to stretch the truth and bend the rules. Such treachery is the result of a fallen race being afraid that it won't be able to stop its descent into mediocrity.

We are in trouble unless we get a greatly needed blood transfusion. Our old (carnal) blood must be exchanged for something new. This happens when we are born again of the Spirit of Jesus Christ. The old stuff is exchanged for new spiritual blood that is applied to our souls (Rom. 3:21-26). Our spirits are regenerated and we experience our new life in Christ, including learning how to be honest.

All of these truths needed to be explained to a man named "George." George and his wife, "Marge," came to me for marriage counseling after his release from prison. I was aware that George's heart was pretty cold and lifeless, bearing witness to the carnal "blood" still there.

In our first session, Marge told me that George had been a brute throughout their marriage. Then she described how things had gotten dramatically worse three years ago when George had landed a new sales job. He spent most evenings back then complaining at her. Looking back, I realize that George had lived with the constant fear that Marge would see him as a failure. Pointing out his wife's flaws had been a devious way of keeping the focus off his own glaring shortcomings.

George had experienced a horrible kind of performance anxiety when he became his division's chief salesman. Crippling fears of underachievement settled into his heart. As a result, he simply couldn't get going on his new job. He felt responsible for so much at the time that he became paralyzed with fear. He began lying about the sales accounts for which he was responsible—trying to keep the boss happy.

When we were alone, George shared how his boss had wanted him to keep a log of the hours spent with respective clients. His record of contacts showed what kind of luck he was having in landing new accounts or beefing up existing ones. His supposed log book became a fairy tale in the making, however. George had no idea how to succeed at his job. He had no idea how to become the super salesman he thought he needed to be. Consequently, the names and places (as well as supposed topics covered) entered in the log book were purely fictitious.

But the lies didn't stop there. George lied to his wife about where he was when he wasn't at the office. Marge would often call to find out what time he would be home for dinner and learn from his secretary that he was out for a sales meeting. When he came home, George had to fabricate the details of all these "meetings"; he couldn't afford to have Marge find out they were a figment of his imagination.

Lying became his way of dealing with imminent failure. He told me that most of his afternoons were spent in a bar instead of on the road chasing down accounts. George thought having a drink would give him the backbone he needed to tell his boss about his predicament. Yet the courage never materialized.

LEARNING TO GET BY

Obviously, a growing dependency on alcohol was robbing him of his ability to function on the job or at home. But I saw his drinking as a symptom rather than the cause of his problems. In our sessions, I began to address the issue of George's "blood type." In the beginning, his blood line had manifested itself through an attitude about "sneaking by" at work. He figured he couldn't do an adequate job at being a top salesperson, which his position demanded. Still, he knew his boss was counting on him. Lying became the perfect solution. George had reasoned that falsifying his log was the only way to make everybody happy. Drinking just became his way of lying to himself about how all of this was going to turn out. Getting home later and later each week (in order to have one more "for the road") had made getting away with all of this seem increasingly easy.

Ultimately, George got around to talking about how he had spent his whole life thinking of himself as a loser. He had done poorly in school and was diagnosed as learning handicapped as a youngster. He had attended special classes throughout elementary school and was horribly embarrassed by other children who labeled him a "retard." Consequently, he felt he would never succeed at anything important. George's ability to land the perfect job had surprised him more than anyone else. That's why it had been easy for him to tell the boss whatever he needed to hear about the looming sales. Meanwhile, he lived in constant fear that he would be recognized as the retard he knew himself to be.

His fear of being seen as incapable was nullified through a false front. It seemed expedient to lie about his weekly contacts with prospective customers. He assumed that sooner or later he would magically land the deal of his life, then everyone would be happy. The problem was, George wasn't meeting that many prospective customers in the bars he was visiting every afternoon.

Time at home was a painful reminder of the emotional distance evolving between him and his wife. Marge was becoming more frustrated with her husband, who either didn't want to talk about things or who would do nothing but complain. In addition, she began receiving calls from George's office asking his whereabouts during the day. When she confronted him, he created another story to explain it all or refused to talk about it. He was digging himself a deeper and deeper hole from which there was no apparent escape.

LUST FOR POWER

To make up for his many lies, more lies had to be crafted. George began cheating the people he served on his existing accounts. He reported bogus sales figures on his monthly inventories. He boosted his figures by showing that these companies were buying larger amounts of goods than was the case. Seeing truly remarkable gross sales figures for the month, his boss was happy. Needless to say, large shipments were returned when these "oversights" were discovered in the shipping and receiving departments involved.

George didn't realize he was seeking power through trickery, while forsaking any chance of purity—the way any of us become men of God and true winners. He decided that the false impression of being a top salesman in his company was the best he could hope for; he had no other means for becoming somebody worth noticing. But God's Word tells us otherwise: "Trust in the Lord, and do good; dwell in the land, and feed on His faithfulness. Delight yourself also in the Lord, and He shall give you the desires of your heart" (Ps. 37:3-4).

Each of us desires to be "something" when we grow up. Achieving an identity is contingent on discovering what we can do to assume importance. The Lord wants us to see that such importance comes by way of trusting in him and doing good. Only then will our dreams be fulfilled and we will amount to anything.

The world thinks it knows better. Its prescription for success invites us to lust for the significance we seek. *Lust* is an Old English word meaning an "overmastering desire, intense enthusiasm, or zest for something." It is born out of a need to possess what we desire at any cost. For those of us who lust for power, cheating is a good way of getting there. George held a lust for power that arose from chronic feelings of failure. Since he couldn't achieve success on his own, he settled for achieving it by way of falsehood. That lust eventually cost him his job and landed him in jail.

No Purity, No Power

Alfred Adler was a famous psychoanalyst of the early 1900s who determined that human beings were involved in a search for meaning that came by way of a "will to power." That power was seen as a source of influence over one's self, as well as others. It was viewed as a measure of a person's ability to know himself and exercise some measure of self-control. This renowned therapist reasoned that self-knowledge would ultimately lead to a clear sense of what was needed by any individual to become truly happy. In this context, happiness was dependent on a neurotically free exercise of the will toward power and influence over the circumstances of one's life.

How nice of humanity to be free of the neurotic ties that bind them to selfishness! All that is required is a soulful search of one's personality dynamics, so a person can be free of anything from his or her past that might darken a rise toward excellence.

What this gifted theorist never understood was that all of humankind has bad blood; their motives are naturally dark. All the hours we might spend on a therapist's couch are pointless if what we seek is purity of heart. Adler was right about one thing, however. Built into all of us is a need to be influential. In general, our attempts to secure power and influence come by way of a need to control things and collect the world's praises. This leads to self-adulation.

Once we become Christians, we are taught that purity of heart is a character quality God is fashioning in our souls. It becomes a divinely inspired attribute allowing us to have power from on high. The Holy Spirit then leads us toward decisions in which the desire to have influence is measured against our awakening need to please the Father and become selfless in the process. Such purity is to be a measure of our willingness to live lives of honor and integrity.

Samson never figured out that his lust for power might cost him his wife's heart—and, very likely, her life. He saw his wife as a thing to possess, not a person deserving his love. Other worldly enterprises called more loudly to Samson, and others' adulation was one of them. We Samsons obviously need to hear praise. Adulation helps reflect our worth in the eyes of the world. Never mind God's grace. A man simply has to accept the idea that "powering up" in this world is the only way to get anywhere. We all have to be top salesmen to achieve some degree of self-satisfaction.

In God's version of a new world order, power must take a backseat to purity. Purity has to do with learning to be content. The blessings the Lord bestows on us need to be appreciated rather than treated contemptuously. Instead of looking for more, we have to learn how to savor what we already have. Such a shift of focus reflects something the Bible identifies as *stewardship*.

A FAITHFUL STEWARD

In Bible times, a steward was responsible for running a household or an estate. He was an administrator of the family's property, money, and any employees. The one principle of good stewardship esteemed above all others was integrity. The steward needed to be somebody the family could trust with the estate.

In a spiritual sense, stewardship must be based on a principle of faithfulness with the things the Lord wishes to give to us (Matt. 25:23). His temporal blessings may include a mate, children, a good paying job, and a simple but lovely one-story house with a nice picket fence. Our job is to appreciate what he has graciously provided, without continuously looking for something newer, brighter, bigger, or better. To accomplish this, we have to examine our potentially covetous hearts from time to time. This will help us stay healthy when the mercury on our spiritual thermometer starts moving toward selfishness.

To accomplish this all-important goal, we must see how well we match the Bible's definition of wise stewardship. Scripture suggests the following: "Love suffers long and is kind; love does not envy; love does not parade itself, is not puffed up; does not behave rudely, does not seek its own, is not provoked, thinks no evil; does not rejoice in iniquity, but rejoices in the truth; bears all things, believes all things, hopes all things, endures all things" (1 Cor. 13:4-7).

Beyond this, Scripture tells us that being loving toward others equates to doing everything without complaining or arguing (Phil. 2:14). We also are to pray—joyfully and continuously—for the individuals God may place on our hearts (1 Thess. 5:17).

Loving our wives as Christ loved the church becomes another of God's exhortations to us about stewardship (Eph. 5:25). This translates into giving our spouses our finest moments and not just the Zzz's we catch once we're at home and on the couch.

Clearly, loving the people God has given us to care about as his stewards of grace requires we not harm them along the way. We need to learn how to carry them through the dry places in their lives, times when they may have nothing to give us in return. Simply put, real love means thinking of someone else's interests before our own (Phil. 2:3).

GETTING A TRANSFUSION

I wish I could say that my great advice got George to see things more clearly. Instead, it was the Lord himself. George came to one of our sessions grinning from ear to ear and saying that his heart had been changed by an experience at church.

He had been listening to his pastor teach on the subject of the Eucharist. The pastor told the congregation that in taking part in Holy Communion (as they were about to do) believers received a kind of spiritual transfusion from on high. George's pastor then read Paul's exhortation to the Corinthian church: "Therefore whoever eats this bread or drinks this cup of the Lord in an unworthy manner will be guilty of the body and blood of the Lord. But let a man examine himself, and so let him eat of that bread and drink of that cup. For he who eats and drinks in an unworthy manner eats and drinks judgment to himself, not discerning the Lord's body" (1 Cor. 11:27-29). George was struck immediately by the relevance of these verses to his own life.

George realized his cheating heart was killing him spiritually. He admitted thinking that Christ's death on the cross was absolutely meaningless unless he saw his own wickedness and stopped being a cheat. As the apostle had warned, George was approaching the Lord's table in an unworthy manner.

That Sunday George had insisted his wife stay home with the kids, so he could go off to church and be alone to pray about things. He assumed this had impressed his wife. But George's real agenda for the morning had been to get off by himself and fashion some new lies about why he hadn't found a new job as yet. While mulling this over in church on this particular Sunday, he suddenly felt horribly convicted about how he was starting to tell lies once more.

Later, as he approached the pastor to receive Communion, George realized he was about to take it unworthily. He needed to acknowledge his selfishness. Only then could he receive Christ's body and blood in a way that would benefit him spiritually. Otherwise, he would remain lifeless inside. In that moment, George asked God's forgiveness.

Acknowledging his heart's insincerity before the Father ensured that the corruption of his human spirit would be drained away. All the while, forgiveness awaited George like an infusion of fresh plasma. His holy transfusion was completed after the service by going to the prayer room and confessing his sin about things at home to a church member. George suddenly felt relieved of the horrible guilt that had gripped him. God's grace was made available in that same moment, as tears began running down his face.

The apostle John once wrote that if we confess our sins to God, he "is faithful and just to forgive us our sins and to cleanse us from all unrighteousness" (1 John 1:9). Confession of this sort involves admitting something about our anemic blood supply that may be killing us. It is an act of wise stewardship pertaining to the vitality of our own souls. In return, God's cleansing power is applied to every aspect of our being. In essence, we get something clean (that is, a pure heart) in exchange for something dirty: our sinful motives and the need to power our way to heaven. It's a deal we can't afford to pass up, especially if we're going to avoid being "guilty of the body and blood of the Lord."

CHRIST'S DEATH IN PRESENT TENSE

The Lord knows about our chronic blood disorder and how it compels us to behave as cheats. Wise stewardship remains impossible for us unless the Lord can purify our hearts and make our spiritual blood supply vital once more. Thankfully, Jesus obtained the secret formula needed to save our hearts from certain corruption. The formula involved exchanging his blood for ours on the Cross (see 1 Pet. 2:24).

Christ donated his blood to the world in order that death would no longer hold people in its grip. Beyond this, the blood that was spilled at Calvary has eternal significance. It is still being applied to our human deficiencies—the moment we turn from sin and admit our need for cleansing.

In taking the Eucharist in a worthy manner, we travel back two thousand years and come to a room where Jesus and his twelve disciples gathered for their last supper together. It was the Passover meal. This meal was instituted by God for the Israelites to commemorate the "passing over" of the death angel on the night they gained their release from Egypt (Exod. 12). God had commanded the Israelites to sprinkle the blood of the lamb slaughtered for the meal on the lintels of the door; this would be a sign that the angel was to pass over those inside the house. Similarly, Jesus' blood covers the lives of his faithful ones. After all, he was the Lamb that was slain to take away the sin of the world.

We repeatedly claim Christ's death as our own through Holy

Communion. The instant we take the bread and wine, Jesus' spiritual wellness can be absorbed into our spirits. The apostle Peter put it this way: "For Christ also suffered once for sins, the just for the unjust, that He might bring us to God, being put to death in the flesh but made alive by the Spirit" (1 Pet. 3:18).

GOD'S READINESS TO FORGIVE

Blood donors give blood so others might live. Jesus did the same thing. Consequently, being wise stewards of our spiritual health means taking advantage of Jesus' blood donation in a timely fashion. For George, this meant going home and telling his wife the truth about what was happening to him. It also involved meeting with his ex-boss several weeks later to finally admit to everything he had done and seek to make financial restitution. This decision came as a result of further conviction by the Holy Spirit when George asked God to forgive him for what he had done to his company.

To George's surprise, not only was God ready to forgive him, so was his boss. He recommended that George pay back all he had cost the company over time. However, he was overjoyed by George's honesty. And he was convinced George was still the man he wanted for the job; he was willing to rehire him for his old position.

Obviously, the outcome to all of this was a "God thing." The heavenly Father's graciousness was made obvious through an outcome George couldn't have imagined in a thousand years. George's heart had been exposed and made well. In addition, he was given the opportunity to pursue a Spirit-led lifestyle that reflected a commitment to purity rather than power—which made him a real winner.

George eventually realized he would have to get his blood cleansed routinely. Taking Communion brought him face to face with God's holiness and his own need for forgiveness. He also joined a men's group at church and confessed his sins there as often as needed. In this new spirit, George volunteered to go to Alcoholics Anonymous and get the help needed to curb his drinking habit. Lastly, he recognized the importance of recommitting himself to his marriage. He agreed to continue in marriage counseling and work at learning how to love his wife sincerely. Ultimately, it seemed that George's blood transfusion meant renewed life for his marriage as much as his own soul.

KEEPING MARRIAGES ALIVE

George's marriage had nearly died because of his ability to lie to himself about what was needed at home. He'd stopped caring about his wife and had become a poor steward of his heart's resources. Love had been replaced with self-interest and the need to get ahead any way necessary.

Many marriages can survive almost total disregard. This is because the business of marriage can go on long after the true relationship has died. But the truth will eventually come out. Poor stewardship will undoubtedly result in the loss of our partner due to our selfishness. Proper stewardship will help us recognize the early warning signs of relational demise. We'll know our marriage is dying because of the constant fighting or the conspicuous absence of words like "I love you." Other signs may include not being able to be in the same room as the other person for more than thirty seconds and not being able to remember the last time we had a real conversation with the person who shares our bed.

Proper stewardship will always include real conversation which goes beyond cliché. Our wives receive an important message in the process. They know they are worth the effort of heartfelt dialogue. We must be genuine in our efforts. That means trying our best to talk at their level, not down or sideways. Lecturing them doesn't count, nor do our feeble attempts to patronize them with gratuitous nods, grunts, and eyes that are glazing over. We need to learn how to talk about important things. Our wives don't need to hear the minute details about our day or get an inventory of how we see the world going down the drain. They want to hear about us—the *feeling* part that seems so unreachable.

Make eye contact. Holding hands is helpful too. It's also good to talk away from distractions (the kids, for instance). And, if such conversations are difficult for us, we must confess our sin of ignorance and do something about it. There is no shame in seeing a marriage counselor who can help us figure out how to talk to one another in a loving manner.

Keeping these things in mind, I have spelled out what commitment to a loving stewardship of our most significant relationships involves:

C = Converse	(Speak eye to eye and heart to heart.)
O = Observe	(Celebrate special times and events such as anniversaries and birthdays.)
M = Memorize	(Say "I love you" repeatedly and tell the other person what you like about him or her. Dwell on these things in your mind.)
M = Mobilize	(Put some effort into the relationship.)
I = Initiate	(Be the one who makes this plan work.)
T = Tantalize and avoid temptation	(Practice making your romantic interludes together exciting. Avoid looking at the ladies when you are with your wife. Better yet, stop looking when you're alone too.)
M = Modernize	(Buy at least two new books on marriage a year—and read them. Don't make your wife pick them out either.)
E = Emotionalize	(Put some feeling into what you're doing.)
N = Normalize	(Don't demand your significant other do anything weird. Weirdness is just a cheater's way of getting by without genuine feelings or concern for his mate.)
T = Tell the truth	(Give up the sham and refuse to pretend that you're really into the relationship. Now start working.)

FINISHING LAST

On a different level, commitment to a life of love and righteousness in our relationship with the world-at-large was spelled out by Paul when he wrote to Timothy: "But you be watchful in all things, endure afflictions, do the work of an evangelist, fulfill your ministry. For I am already being poured out as a drink offering, and the time of my departure is at hand. I have fought the good fight, I have finished the race, I have kept the faith" (2 Tim. 4:5-7).

The race in which we are involved is one of faith. Remember, Point B is our final destination. Paul could say just before his death that he had "finished the race" and found his way to a lasting faith. Such faith involved a purity of heart and a kind of integrity that allowed God's divine purpose to be fulfilled in his life.

Scripture declares that at the end of the age, there is going to be a glorious feast given for those of us who have chosen to run this race of endurance. It will be a celebration for those of us who have remained faithful to God's command to be wise stewards of all that he has given us. I'm afraid cheaters aren't going to be on the invitation list (see Matt. 22:1-14). To cross the finish line, we must give up being self-serving thieves. Instead, we must learn how to let the people in our lives assume more significance than ourselves. This is how we can be certain of a strong finish and guarantee the health of our spiritual blood throughout the race. Jesus told us as much when he reminded us that "the last will be first, and the first last" (Matt. 20:16).

The following checklist offers one way of checking up on the wellness of our hearts. Use it to examine your heart when you're struggling to get along with the person next door, at the office, or wherever. If followed faithfully, it will help you end up the winner in any conflict. The secret of our hearts' wellness rests in our choosing to let the other guy be first while we practice being number two in the race for significance.

"THE LAST WILL BE FIRST" CHECKLIST

- Have I prayed about this situation asking "What am I doing wrong here, Lord? How am I blowing it with this person?"

- Have I gone to the Bible to see how I might handle things differently? Am I willing to look at what it says about the spirit I'm operating in or how I need to change?

- Have I asked anyone for godly counsel or feedback as to what my part in all of this should be?

- Am I willing to listen to what the other person is trying to tell me *about me?*

- Am I willing to compromise and settle for a practical solution that allows everybody involved a chance to feel understood and appreciated? Or do I have a need to be "right," so that giving in is impossible? Am I striving to do the most loving thing I can do (given the circumstance), even if that means losing the argument?

This selfless approach to relationships is not natural to us. As Samsons in this world, we tend to settle for power as the means for getting ahead in life. But living a life of faith entails surrendering the need to power our way to success, and through God's Holy Spirit, purify our hearts instead.

THINGS TO THINK ABOUT AND DO

1. Think about some time you've spent in prayer recently (or trying to read the Word) when you felt like you were getting nowhere. Write out some possible reasons for the sense of ineffectiveness you felt. Begin by asking yourself if you are holding any grudges toward anyone. What ways may you be trying to cheat in acting

loving toward the people in your life? Confess whatever sin the Lord brings to mind—first to him and then to the people in question, if that seems reasonable to do.

2. Look again at the acrostic on commitment spelled out on page 146. If you are married, list the ways you feel you are currently falling short in trying to live up to your commitment to your wife. Make a plan for recommitment and start keeping a weekly log of the ways you've tried to show your love to your wife. If you aren't married, make an acrostic of your own that reflects how to be a more loving person. Write down your successes or failures in trying to live up to your definition.

3. Using the "Last Will Be First Checklist" as a guide, describe a recent conflict and how the situation might have been improved had you used the checklist. Then write a letter to the person with whom you were fighting and admit how you might have been wrong in your attitude about things. Chance asking him or her for forgiveness and try moving toward reconciliation.

10

PURSUING GOD'S PRESENCE

A s created beings, we are designed to be spiritually attached in order to feel whole. For this reason, we have been granted an innate hunger to search out our Creator's existence. This need takes on paramount importance for our sense of well-being.

The problem is that God remains outside our view in a very big universe. Being blind to his whereabouts, we might wonder if he hasn't disappeared altogether. Added to this fear is the realization that God is entirely different from us. We are temporal in nature, made of flesh and blood. He occupies an invisible realm and is Spirit. How can we successfully cross the barrier between these two realities—the visible and the invisible?

We men trapped by a Samson-like personality will conjure up any number of brainless ideas for getting close to God. We settle for human sentiment as a measure of God's proximity. We wrongfully assume that if we can't see the Lord, maybe we can at least "feel" him in some way; then we'll know we're moving in the right direction. Unfortunately, the realm of touchy-feely emotions just isn't going to help.

GETTING BEYOND THE GOOSE BUMPS

Being sentimental can get us into a heap of trouble when it to comes to spying out God. Emotionalism may color our perceptions, and

God's Spirit may get lost in the frenzy. Spiritual discernment, on the other hand, allows us to experience the eternal presence of our heavenly Father—free of wishful thinking. Discernment aids our ability to hang in there with the Lord because we can recognize his good work in our lives (Rom. 8:28).

The biggest problem many Christians face in developing discernment is the religious world we occupy. Here, faith and the visitation of the Holy Spirit are often defined according to the number of goose bumps they raise. As long as we can see miraculous sights, utter strange sounds, fall down on cue, or work up a holy sweat for the Lord, we'll be certain that it's God we're clinging to.

Samson clearly showed his preference for goose bumps as a believer. After wreaking havoc on the Philistines at Ashkelon, Samson's adrenalin rush was mistaken for God's anointing. As a result, "his anger was aroused, and he went back up to his father's house. And Samson's wife was given to his companion, who had been his best man" (Judg. 14:19-20). Samson looked to his parents to smooth things over at home, but he was too late. The divorce papers were already signed and his "ex" was now in the arms of another man. Any intuition he had about people was lost to his need to let impulse rule his heart. He apparently believed that his murderous rages were purely understandable—given that he vented them in the name of Jehovah God. Meanwhile, Samson lost the ability to truly understand God's will for his life.

His father-in-law desperately tried to explain how his behavior toward his wife had left everyone with the impression he hated her (see Judg. 15:2). As a result, Dad tried pawning off the woman's sister to this big crybaby—just to keep Samson from erupting once more. Samson would have nothing to do with a peaceful settlement.

In our day, Samson would be considered a "rage-aholic." Malice aforethought ruled his heart. When things went sour for him, he rampaged. Samson got childishly mad, stayed mad, and blamed everybody else. Now his anger led him to set the Philistine wheat fields aflame, along with the local vineyards and anything else combustible.

The Philistines were not to be outdone. They lived up to their promise to get even with Samson's wife by setting her father's house on fire. She was consumed in the inferno. Tragically, Samson's rage-aholic nature caught up with him, and somebody else paid the price.

THE ADULT-CHILD GROWS UP

Samson's emotional problems can probably be summed up in one hyphenated word: *adult-child*. The adult-child is someone who has never grown up. He tends to be overly dependent on others and tries to hide the fact that he is emotionally stunted. He will usually seek out other adult-children whose codependency issues compel them to rescue such people from the rigors of life. The adult-child and his codependent partner limp along toward an adulthood that is never achieved, using each other for a crutch.

By attaching ourselves to someone who allows us to be a child, we don't have to worry about growing up. On the contrary, we decide that the Holy Spirit's invitation to grow up in him can be negotiated some other time. We have a lost childhood to catch up on first.

This emotional predicament often results from the dysfunctional homes in which we were raised. Our families of origin represented laboratories where our parents modeled their own infantile natures. Having been denied healthy adult role models to emulate, we have a fearful bewilderment over our future roles. Our concept of maleness gets twisted into a belief that codependency is a must. Along with it come a goodly amount of denial, avoidance, power, and mind control.

God's solution is simple. It is called "Christ-dependency." Such dependency is the only means for discerning God's holy presence. Looking to the Lord Jesus to meet our deepest human needs ensures that we will become adult-children of God. In this context, Jesus models the righteousness we need to be healthy adults and our spiritual lives become fruitful, thereby glorifying the Father.

BEARING GOOD FRUIT

Being fruitful means living our lives in a way that pleases the Lord. But unless we become totally reliant on Christ, we won't be able to bear anything tasty for the kingdom. (Jesus told his followers this very thing. In John 15:5 he explained that he was the vine and they were the branches; remaining in him would mean his disciples would bear much fruit.)

Being fruitful doesn't just happen, however. We have to practice being individuals who bear good fruit for Jesus. In the process, our ignorance about adulthood will be replaced by a sense of understanding of what growing up in Christ looks like. To this end, I have come up with a simple list of how to bear good fruit. It involves discerning the fruit of the Spirit and living accordingly (see Gal. 5:22-23).

- Be loving, caring about someone when it would be easier to turn away.

- Be joyful, smiling even when being sad might seem more justified or gain you the greatest sympathy.

- Be peaceful, being the first one to give in, no matter who's right.

- Be patient, working to understand others' shortcomings and failures while restraining your own anger.

- Be kind, showing deference to those who oppose you.

- Be good, choosing not to sin even when you know you can get away with it.

- Be faithful, practicing devotion when ignoring it might give you the advantage.

■ Be gentle, avoiding intimidation.

■ Be self-controlled, giving up the negative habits that control you.

"Jim" was a graduate student who came to counseling to talk about his roommate "Tom." He and Tom had rented an apartment together in their first semester of graduate school, with Jim fronting the money for the security deposit. In just the second semester of their studies, Tom hurried home one afternoon to tell Jim he was getting married the next week. The woman was somebody Tom had met the first day of class. Good for Tom, bad for Jim: he was left to pay off the lease on the apartment they shared.

Out of a desire to remain friends, Jim decided to stay in contact with Tom after his marriage. This was in spite of the fact Jim had not even been invited to the wedding; Tom and his new bride chose to run to Las Vegas to get married. Now, Jim was sitting in my office trying to sort out his feelings. In particular, he was upset over how Tom played the part of helpless victim while getting other people to rescue him.

Another quirk of Tom's bugged Jim almost as much. Tom assumed he was Spirit-filled and knew something about the workings of God's Spirit. As proof, he was constantly demonstrating his prayer language in the university church they had attended together. Tom also was convinced he had a gift of healing because he felt a strange kind of heat coming from his palms whenever he stretched them out toward people. He leaped at the opportunity to usher new converts into the kingdom by laying his trembling hands upon them. This occurred whenever visitors would respond to the pastor's invitation to come forward and make a public profession of their faith. Jim laughed as he told me how Tom knew when God was working through him: the hair on the back of his neck stood up.

TOUCHY-FEELY DOESN'T WORK

In spite of his spiritual fervor at church, Tom remained a rebel. Jim described him as being sexually promiscuous prior to his marriage. All the while, Tom insisted God would forgive his moral lapses. After all, Tom was "on fire for the Lord"; a few improprieties would be overlooked. He apparently approached his marriage with the same mindset. Any shortcomings as a husband could be ignored as long as Tom remained a churchgoing, Spirit-filled man who accomplished something great for God's kingdom. Sadly, Tom's marriage was soon a disaster, and he lost the apartment his parents had set up for him and his new wife. He asserted that his inability to keep a job or pay the rent was mostly the result of his needing to spend more time hitting the books in order to graduate.

Meanwhile, Tom was always approaching Jim for a loan, and Jim felt awkward in saying no. When he did, Tom's parents helped him out of any problems he faced. Tom also looked to his in-laws for support whenever he and his wife encountered a new financial crisis. The fact that he spent money like crazy and kept getting fired from his many part-time jobs made everyone's help an ongoing necessity.

What seemed strange to Jim was that Tom's parents never got around to asking him where he spent all the money he kept borrowing. Only later did Jim find out that Tom's money problems were mostly the result of a drug habit he couldn't kick. That bit of information led Jim finally to confront Tom about his apparent selfishness, and he swore to never help him again.

Jim came to me to find out what he "ought" to be feeling. I assured him that any and all feelings were probably legitimate in this situation. In particular, I helped him see that his anger at Tom for his supposed fervor for the Lord was his most understandable feeling. God himself has said that, rather than burnt offerings or rivers of oil, what he requires of us is "to do justly, to love mercy, and to walk humbly with your God" (see Mic. 6:7-8).

Tom's touchy-feely way of relating to God was useless. His soul was dying along a path of "charismania" and he was taking his loved ones along for the ride. Ironically, everybody's willingness to bail Tom out of any and all messes made growing up completely unnecessary for him. Staying spiritually prepubescent was far easier than facing the rigors of life.

THE BY-PRODUCT OF A CHILDISH MIND

Fear forces us Samsons to hide our childish hearts away. We surely don't want anyone noticing we aren't old enough to take care of ourselves. For Tom, drugs became a way out of a marriage he didn't know what to do with. Foolishly, sentiment in the pew on Sundays helped convince him God approved of his plan. And, somewhere in his childish mind was the thought that his parents would always save him, if necessary.

Soon after my first session with Jim, he telephoned me. He had gotten a phone call from Tom telling him he was in jail. Tom wanted Jim to bail him out; he was too embarrassed to call his parents. Jim agreed, but only if Tom was willing to come see me. Not wanting to spend another night behind bars, Tom said okay. Our therapeutic relationship began the next week.

Tom was nervous in our first meeting. He awkwardly told me of how he was arrested for possession and being "under the influence." His DUI involved plowing his mother's new car into another car on the freeway. The girl whose car he had struck was in the hospital with serious injuries. He sheepishly admitted the accident was strictly his fault. He had been distracted while lighting up a joint and hadn't noticed the car in front of him coming to a sudden stop.

I suggested that at the very moment he was placed behind bars, the Lord had begun a new work in him. I invited Tom to see his predicament as a wake-up call from the Lord. He liked this idea because it helped him begin feeling something besides dread. Tom confessed he was frightened for the first time in his life. Lovingly, I pointed out that fear can sometimes be healthy for us—"the fear of the Lord is the beginning of wisdom" (Prov. 9:10).

Tom also admitted that, for the first time in his life, he had cried out to God (from his cell) with no real certainty that the Lord would respond. Strangely, God's mercy was now seen as a gift and not a "thank you." Reality was setting in for Tom as to what a Spirit-filled life was all about. It meant searching for the Lord with all of his heart—rather than by way of the hair on the back of his neck.

THE CAPACITY TO DISCERN

God's solution to a problem such as Tom's is to help us become an adult-child of God who recognizes his Father's presence. God's kingdom must be seen as real, which requires a living faith that doesn't rely on a touchy-feely way of doing things or the codependency that defines our existence. The apostle Paul put it this way:

> Now we have received, not the spirit of the world, but the Spirit who is from God, that we might know the things that have been freely given to us by God. These things we also speak, not in words which man's wisdom teaches but which the Holy Spirit teaches, comparing spiritual things with spiritual. But the natural man does not receive the things of the Spirit of God, for they are foolishness to him; nor can he know them, because they are spiritually discerned. (1 Cor. 2:12-14)

Only the Lord has the power to help us see his eminence. Through the gift of discernment, we are granted the privilege of seeing and understanding the workings of God who is Spirit. This kind of "Spirit vision" doesn't require 3-D glasses, just the ability to (1) see God's timing in our lives, with regard to his grace and (2) hear his prophetic voice.

SEEING GOD'S TIMING

In order to feel like we are getting close to God, we have to be able to take note of his promises and capitalize on them. These promises represent the manifestation of his grace and allow his Spirit to materialize right before our very eyes. Otherwise, we end up feeling alone because God's goodness and mercy never become an experiential reality.

God's desire is to shower us with spiritual gifts, material blessings, or opportunities that are ours for the taking. All we have to do is be able to see (or spiritually discern) their timing and respond to God's invitation to partake of his favor. The risk of not recognizing these special moments was spoken of by the author of Hebrews. He warned that if we don't act on God's promises, then the time of God's rest will pass us by (Heb. 3:7-15). A golden opportunity will be missed, as will a sense of God's whereabouts.

Tom came to one of our sessions with an intriguing story that proved this point. He told me about a "chance encounter" he had had with another member of his church just prior to his arrest. He said he had been high at the time, so he hadn't given much credence to their conversation at the time. Now he was ready to reevaluate what had happened.

A girl from his church had apparently walked up to him on campus and simply said, "I've been praying and fasting for you and feel led to tell you that time is running out." She had just as quickly apologized for sharing this "word" in such an awkward manner. She admitted she didn't know what any of this meant, only that the prompting of the Lord had been unbearable. She acknowledged she had spent weeks agonizing over whether she would even talk to Tom the next time she saw him. But, at the moment they crossed paths, she knew she had to say something.

Only later did Tom see the relevance and timing of God's message to him. His drug use was ultimately going to destroy him, just as it had nearly cost someone else her life. Since God hadn't gotten Tom's attention through the word that was spoken to him that day on campus, the Lord decided to get his attention in a more circuitous manner.

Jail time served Tom well in this regard because it represented a golden moment for quiet reflection. During Tom's darkest hours—sitting in a lonely concrete cell—the lights suddenly went on in his spirit. There was a dawning awareness that his relationship with the

Lord had always been superficial. In addition, he could see how his attitude about his wife and marriage was equally shallow. He had some growing up to do.

Those three days in jail provided Tom with the impetus to review every aspect of his life. The only thing an inmate has going for him is time and Tom made use of every second. He decided to begin telling the truth—to himself—about the kind of person he was. In allegorical fashion, Tom wrote a short story called "The Man Who Never Learned to Be Real" and read it to me in my office. The story showed how Tom had been emotionally adrift all his life. He also told of never feeling close to God. In the final paragraphs of his story, Tom acknowledged that his parents' willingness to always be there for him had been a large part of the problem. Tom knew he had been kept an infant, and he resented the implications. Still, he refused to blame them for their misgivings in raising him. Doing so was only going to keep him a kid a little longer.

HEARING GOD'S VOICE

Beyond seeing God's timing, discernment requires we learn how to hear God's prophetic voice. Discernment gives us an ability to listen with our hearts, in order to recognize where the Lord is leading us. In the process, our underlying fears of estrangement die away.

God likes to speak to our spirits in a relatively quiet manner. He does this through his providence, prophetic utterances, our consciences, and Scripture.

God's providence in our lives is the spiritual scorecard we keep in our minds as we assess whether we're in step with God. Success keeps us moving, while failure usually makes us stop and think about things. Constant failure may be God's providential way of indicating that he has turned in another direction, and we need to get back in line with his will.

Prophetic utterance is a mysterious source of divine revelation in which the Lord gets our attention by delivering a specific message through an emissary. Such "words of knowledge" often will surprise us by their intimacy and their ability to touch on the very problem we are currently facing. These utterances (such as those spoken to Tom by the girl on campus) are obviously meant to clue us in on things.

Conscience represents another vehicle for godly pronouncements. The Lord "speaks" to us through a quiet inner voice inside our heads. When we consider doing things that we aren't certain carry God's blessing, some still, small voice inside will impress us to stop. God's Word says that all of us have been given a conscience so that we might know the difference between right and wrong (see Rom. 1:18-25).

Obviously, our conscience is not foolproof (see 1 Tim. 4:2). Hence, the Father supplies us with an infallible source of divine revelation—the Bible. We read: "For the word of God is living and powerful, and sharper than any two-edged sword, piercing even to the division of soul and spirit, and of joints and marrow, and is a discerner of the thoughts and intents of the heart" (Heb. 4:12). When the Holy Spirit brings us to a point of conviction through God's written Word, we won't be able to escape its gnawing effects on our spirits.

Soon after his arrest, Tom received a paperback version of the New Testament. He discovered that the Word sprang to life in a new way over the three days he was stuck in jail. God wanted Tom to be done with his drug life. Tom was certain of this. Hence, the Word was brought down like Excalibur upon his intellect's view of things. Verses on the importance of the purity of marital love also caught his ear and pained his soul. He realized his thinking about drugs was simply wrong, as were his disparaging thoughts of his marriage.

Sitting in his cell, Tom found out his heavenly Father's quiet voice had a way of sneaking past his excuses. While Tom may have been expecting an earthquake, the Lord slipped in the back door of his heart with his divine sword drawn.

SAYING NO TO THE FLESH

Being Christ-dependent also involves learning how to say no to our many carnal appetites. Our hunger for attachment and an ensuing identity needs to be directed toward the invisible hem of Jesus' garment rather than the tangibles of this world. Otherwise, we will be infants driven by impulse, whose understanding of the deep things of God will be shallow at best. Discernment will seem impossible for us.

God's prescription involves abstention. It is the way of personal sacrifice and self-denial in giving up the right to the relief of our worldly appetites. It is called *fasting* and it breaks up our heart's indifference toward the things of God.

A fast forces us into starving our flesh so our spirits can finally be fed. God's Word tells us that when we seek the Lord with all of our hearts, we will find him (Deut. 4:29). Doing that requires we have a heart hungry enough to go looking for him in the first place. One means of establishing this kind of hunger is through a Spirit-led fast (Joel 1:13-15).

Fasting puts us in touch with how dependent on God we really are. By the power of choice, we adopt a posture in the world that reflects the very truth we have been trying to avoid: we are spiritually small and cannot feed ourselves. Thus, hunger becomes a sobering experience that brings us to the edge of our feelings of vulnerability. When we stop depending on temporal sustenance, we have to start depending on an invisible God who promises to be there in some mystical sort of way. Only then can true reliance on the Lord—Christ-dependency—begin.

STARVING THE ADULT TO FEED THE CHILD

Tom decided to go on a five-day fast upon my recommendation. I figured that a fast had helped the woman he met on campus hear the Lord's voice; a fast of his own might accomplish the same thing. Besides, Tom needed to do something to get himself out of the

spiritual rut he was in. A fast was a perfect means for him to com-
municate his newfound desire to live life God's way. I decided to
join him; fasts carried out in partnership with someone else can be
a powerful means of hearing the Lord's voice.

After a week, we met to compare notes. Tom admitted that
during the first three days of eating nothing, he began to squirm
inside. He didn't realize it would be this difficult. I assured him
that spiritual forces beyond his reckoning were being moved out
of the way. There definitely was a battle going on inside of him.
He had spent his whole life looking for the easy way out. Now
there would be pain.

Fasting brought Tom's control problems to the surface. After two
days, he had a horrible headache. He missed his sugar supply something awful, not to mention the drugs. After four days, he began
trying to figure out how to cheat on his fast. He was miserable but
knew he needed to keep going. He was irritable, depressed, and
hopeless.

A fast is effective in moving obstacles such as bitterness or rage
out of the way in our hearts. These obstacles represent the hardening
we feel in our capacity for being loving. Bitterness over how life
has turned out will do that to the best of us, turning us to stone if
left untreated. In biblical terms, we will suffer from a fallow heart.
A Spirit-led fast can break up a fallow heart and create within us
a newfound ability to care about the people around us. The prophet
Isaiah suggested, "Is this not the fast that I [the Lord] have chosen:
to loose the bonds of wickedness, to undo the heavy burdens, to
let the oppressed go free, and that you break every yoke?"
(Isa. 58:6).

Tom's yoke had to do with a highly destructive anger that manifested itself in his marriage. He admitted that his rages led him to
break things to get his wife to listen to him, and she was very
intimidated by him. Such anger needs to be identified and resisted
with all our heart. Otherwise, it will consume us—just as it did
Samson. Resisting this form of anger begins the moment we can
admit it exists. Its form generally looks like this:

■ Aggression (whether physical or emotional) against another, which is born out of a need to be "on top" or in control.

■ A need to deny any wrongdoing.

■ Giving in to destructive impulses because controlling them involves time and effort.

■ Expecting things to go our way. This equates to being selfish but not wanting to admit it.

■ Relating to the world as a child (that is, throwing tantrums rather than learning how to talk things out).

A SPIRITUAL BREAKTHROUGH

Tom began to change when he finally saw how destructive his anger had become and how closely he fit the profile of a batterer. As a result, his fallow heart began to loosen. He started seeing how much contempt there was inside for anybody who wanted to control him, especially women. He also saw how much suspicion there was toward his wife because it seemed she was potentially very powerful.

Tom's fast produced a sudden need to talk. He reflected on his past and where his many fears about manhood had originated. For example, he described his father as a "rager" who was physically abusive while Mom was determined to keep peace at any cost. She would cower whenever Tom's father began to scream at her and push her around, doing nothing to escape this situation. She also acquiesced to her husband's need to ram his fists through the walls of their home.

In talking about all of this, Tom felt remorse for his parents. All they could do to hide their own ignorance, fear, and infantile natures was never demand anything from him. Chores were never thought of and responsibilities were nonexistent. All that was expected of Tom was that he join his parents in going to church every Sunday.

While his parents barely spoke at times, occasional "revivals" were made the holy remedy for the carnage at home. Tears came when he could finally admit he didn't have a Mom or Dad who could show him the way to adulthood. Tom had been alone and afraid throughout his childhood and hated it.

Now, he didn't need to feel afraid any longer. He could begin to face life as a man because he was beginning to appreciate God's presence in a new way. Through a fast that revealed the emptiness inside, Tom was able to see that the Holy Spirit was available to render first aid.

Tom was more than ready. First, we grieved together for the loss of his childhood. Next, I had Tom and his wife enroll in a weekend marriage-enrichment seminar sponsored through their church. In addition, I had him promise to spend six months reading some Christian books on men's and women's issues. Finally, I asked him to join a men's group that a partner of mine was running at the time. Because Tom was given probation, he was able to follow through with these recommendations. Out of this soul-searching came lasting healing for Tom and his marriage. He was free to discern God's will for his life.

STEPS FOR FASTING

Tom's revelatory changes were spawned by a fast. Fasting allows the Lord to knead the dough of our human spirit. He rolls us around on the inside, flattens us out, then rolls us up once more. He works the ingredients of his *agape* love into our hearts, and the bitterness begins to disappear. Real spiritual hunger begins to replace the temporary pangs of immediate need gratification, as we discover that the pain inside our souls can find release.

Let me offer you my formula for a fast. It isn't meant to meet every challenge that might be offered against its theological accuracy; it's simply a means of determining our readiness (or hunger) to change. Please check with your doctor first. If certain health problems dictate against a food fast, then other things can be substituted. The most important thing to keep in mind is that it's our earnestness in seeking God's will that is being challenged, not our ability to lose weight.

- Select a time frame of duration in which starvation of the soul is bound to hurt. Most importantly, don't fast for the right "look" but for the right results.

- Select a substance or activity (for example, food, sex, TV) dear to your heart and offer it to the Lord as a genuine form of sacramental love and obedience "unto repentance" (2 Cor. 7:10). If thinking about giving something up temporarily makes you nervous, you're on the right track.

- Ask the Lord for discernment in showing you the areas in your life that represent a fallow heart. List ways you have become hardened to things and what attitudes need to be surrendered during your fast.

- Ask the Lord to show you how to become more Christ-dependent by reading his Word daily.

- Allow yourself a time of praise and worship daily. This provides your spirit with the company of the Holy Spirit, for the Lord inhabits the praises of his people (Ps. 22:3). Read from the Psalms or try singing some of your favorite hymns or choruses from church. If you can't sing, turn up your CD player and go for it with one of your gospel favorites.

It takes courage and faith to pursue God through the discernment of his Spirit rather than relying on our own human sentiment. But our faith is built up as we accept the challenge to starve our immediate physical needs. We will discover that we're not alone in the universe after all. God is with us, ready to provide spiritual nourishment.

TRUE MANHOOD

Jesus is the male role model to whom we must attach to experience a lasting sense of identity in the Spirit. In Jesus' life on earth, we have the best example ever offered of what being a man is all about. Therefore, I would recommend that we search the Gospels and become familiar with Jesus' style of relating to both men and women. Writing out our impressions and incorporating them in a synopsis of Christlike character will prove helpful.

We will discover Jesus was always kind, direct, sensitive to the needs of others, and dependent on the Father for everything. He wasn't codependent with anyone and never manipulated to get his way. He prayed constantly and showed a genuine dependence on God. Even though he left his heavenly kingdom behind, Jesus discovered a sense of belonging here on earth by accurately perceiving the Father's invisible presence. He could discern God's presence by having the eyes and ears of his heart attuned to the Father's will and direction for his life. As we pursue God with our whole hearts, we too will find a true sense of belonging and purpose.

THINGS TO THINK ABOUT AND DO

1. Study Jesus' interactions with men and women. Examine how he approached each of the sexes and write down your impressions of any differences. Do some reading on topics related to the opposite sex and spend time trying to familiarize yourself with how God works to empower each sex to make his Body complete on earth.
2. Ask yourself in what ways you may be codependent with someone. This person will very likely be the person who puts up with everything you do to them and tries to fix you all the while. What would life be like if you didn't have them to lean on anymore? Try being honest about your codependency and share your revelation with this person. Then, join a support group where

codependency is discussed and alternatives toward healthy relationships are explored.

3. Think about things you might want to give up for a while in seeking the Lord's presence. Follow the outline above and try to surrender your heart to the Lord for a thorough examination. In what ways do you think it might be fallow or need to be changed? Write out your impressions, then write a prayer asking for God's help in softening you up.

4. If you are a rager, admit your problem right away. Seeking help is a must—for your own sake as well as for others'. For example, get the help you need by enrolling in an anger management program as soon as possible. Such programs are available through local mental health agencies. I also would recommend you seek out a counselor in order to make yourself accountable to someone. Let this choice to be responsible launch a period of healing.

11

GRACE OR GUTS?

We have one last category of angst to explore together. It has to do with our need for reward in this life. This is because the accumulation of wealth (or something else we can possess) becomes a measure of our "okay-ness" with God. So we start relying on the goodies of this life to measure our success and approval in God's eyes.

From God's point of view, passing the grade means accepting his unmerited favor for our lives. God's grace toward us more than proves we are acceptable to him. The Bible clearly says that God is able to meet all of our needs through the "riches in glory" that are available in Christ Jesus (Phil. 4:19). Those riches are supplied through God's grace in a particular manner—by way of prayer.

GUTS COUNT FOR EVERYTHING

Prayer helps us see that we don't have to make it on our own in this world. The Lord is ready to meet our every need in offering his divine protection, guidance, and mercy upon request. But don't expect our culture to tell you this. Rather, the world around us testifies that if we work hard at getting ahead and believe in ourselves, we can make our dreams come true. Who needs grace when guts count for everything?

The movie *Rocky* exemplified this point perfectly. As a has-been prizefighter, Rocky was everybody's friend and a ready-made sucker. Yet, he discovered that in accepting a challenge and learning how to believe in himself, he could accomplish anything he wanted.

The turning point in the story comes when Rocky is invited to fight the heavyweight champion of the world. The champ figures he can whip Rocky blindfolded. But, for Rocky, the fight is his chance to prove himself. Although Rocky had felt like a loser all of his life, his manager knew he had more going for him. The manager just had to convince "Rock" of the same thing.

Toward the end of the picture, Rocky is slumping in his corner after fourteen rounds of grueling battering, barely able to breath. His face resembles hamburger, and everyone figures he is going to be lucky just to answer the bell for the last round. But Rocky has come too far to quit now. Just before the final bell sounds, his manager is yelling encouragement and the crowd is on its feet, screaming, "Rocky! Rocky! Rocky!"

At the bell, Rocky is on his feet and plodding to the center of the ring, ready to meet his rival. Everything is different now. The deadness in his eyes has vanished and hope is blossoming. Rocky has gotten it: the human will can save the day and one's dreams as well. He realizes he can do the impossible because success is mostly about self-will. With this new truth tucked away in his heart, Rocky stands up to the champ.

HUMANISM'S MANIFESTO

Rocky's view of things represents the humanistic manifesto of our time. It suggests that if you believe in yourself sincerely enough, you can do anything. It's a great story line for a Hollywood flick, but its conclusion is fallacious. Going back out there for the final round simply believing in yourself only proves one thing: you're pretty dumb.

Jesus knew this and provided ample warning by saying to the "tough-it-outers" of his day, "And whoever falls on this stone [meaning Christ] will be broken; but on whomever it falls, it will grind him to powder" (Matt. 21:44). Jesus was telling us that unless we throw in the towel on ourselves, we're going to lose as participants in the fight that life poses. Our struggle for a final reward of some kind—whether recognition, riches, or worldly influence—will result in us getting pulverized instead. The enemy of our faith will be able to put us down for the count.

Satan's best punch is aimed at our hearts. He delivers it by convincing us to live by rules of self-indulgence in gaining the rewards we seek. According to his fight plan, greed is crucial. It combats all those fears we have over losing out on the spoils of this existence. Thus, we enter the ring with the thought that "he who dies with the most toys wins."

The Lord knows all about the enemy's fight plan. That's why he wants to put on the gloves and square off against Satan on our behalf. For "the battle is the Lord's, and He will give [the enemy] into our hands" (1 Sam. 17:47). Being men, however, may mean going out there to prove we can do it ourselves. The false self never wants to pass up a chance to shine. The battle lines get drawn, and we have to decide how to enter the fray. We can march out there like Rocky—believing in ourselves—or, we can let Jesus enter the ring for us and allow his grace to shine.

GOING IT ALONE

Samson never gave God a second thought when it came to a fight. He was determined to go it alone. The day he avenged his bride's murder, God's unmerited favor didn't seem that essential; Samson seemed to be doing pretty well on his own. He attacked the murderers with "great slaughter" and immediately felt better about things (Judg. 15:7-8). While grieving might have been appropriate, sadness wasn't something he had time for. Real men don't cry, remember.

The danger of allowing falsehood to show us how to survive is that we never learn how to talk to God. Who needs to talk when we have the world by the tail? We presume God's input isn't that important while waiting for our natural strengths and talents to save the day. Because of this quirk of our male nature, we are destined to fall. We topple like a statue and break into a thousand pieces—and Satan is waiting with the dust pan.

Samson didn't want to talk to God because he didn't want to have to look inside. He might have had to admit to some feelings about his wife's murder. Being the strong and silent type, he went to live near Elam, hoping God wouldn't bother him further (see Judg. 15:8). Undoubtedly, Samson was struggling with anguish and grief. Prayer would have helped. Instead, his soul was tortured by what it was feeling, having been responsible for his wife's death.

Three thousand of Samson's fellow Israelites arrived at Elam and convinced him to give himself up. Then they attempted to turn him over to the Philistine cutthroats looking for him. They figured they had removed this outlaw from their midst, along with any likelihood of a Philistine reprisal (Judg. 15:13).

Under the circumstances, God's prescription would have been a dose of conviction for Samson. This would have helped him find his way to God's loving arms and protection. Condemnation was all that Samson heard within his spirit, however. This happens when we stop talking to the Lord and start hiding. Guilt sets in because a profound truth escapes us in our silence. The truth is that the Father is always ready to receive us, no matter what we've done or how messy our lives have become. God's Word tells us as much: "Therefore [Jesus] is also able to save to the uttermost those who come to God through Him, since He ever lives to make intercession for them" (Heb. 7:25).

False pride often gets in the way of something so simple. Staying quiet about the pain inside means we can continue to be seen as men. Tragically, our silence forces us out of the Lord's care and into the arms of the enemy.

LEARNING TO ACCEPT HELP

Samson was definitely acting like an ass, and God wanted him to see this point. So, the Lord delivered him from danger once more through the jawbone of a donkey. (Does God have a sense of humor or what?) We read:

> When he came to Lehi, the Philistines came shouting against him. Then the Spirit of the Lord came mightily upon him; and the ropes that were on his arms became like flax that is burned with fire, and his bonds broke loose from his hands. He found a fresh jawbone of a donkey, reached out his hand and took it, and killed a thousand men with it. (Judg. 15:14-15)

Following his one-man military campaign, Samson let go of pride long enough to pray. He actually admitted he needed something from Jehovah, asking him to quench his thirst. God obliged by splitting a rock in two; out poured a stream of water (Judg. 15:18-19).

By typology, the Lord was introducing Samson to his Son Jesus. The image of water pouring from a broken rock speaks of God's desire to pour out his mercy and grace through the Rock of our salvation. God had shared this mighty truth with Moses years before. Moses was instructed to strike the rock at Horeb, so that God's people might receive the refreshment they needed to survive their desert wanderings (see Exod. 17). The rock symbolized God's Son who was to be broken for humanity on the cross at Calvary as an outpouring of God's love on a dying world. Prayer brings us to the Rock of our salvation, where we can receive God's favor once more. By turning to Jesus, we discover he is the Living Water we need to quench our thirst for comfort, peace, and lasting joy.

BREAKING THE SILENCE

Dealing with real feelings through prayer is mandatory if we are to make it to Point B and a lasting faith in the Lord. After all, the one thing life ensures us is that we're going to suffer setbacks and losses. Losing dreams, hopes, expectations, and relationships seems to be what our time on earth is meant to teach us about surviving. Consequently, refreshment and renewal are needed to survive our own desert wanderings.

For this reason, baring our souls to the Lord in prayer is essential. Often, this includes doing much-needed grieving, by which our silent acrimony, guilt, or shame can be removed. Our silence over how much we hurt must be exchanged for the soothing reassurance that our Savior will get us through even the most painful times. We simply must be willing to voice our emotions earnestly to the Lord.

Grief work of this kind entails passing through any number of highs and lows in our emotional lives. After the shock of our loss has worn off, we have to work through our denial. Then, anger and hurt will surface. Next, we may get stuck trying to bargain our way out of having to deal with any of it.

My mother discovered this fact after my father's suicide. She never cried over my father's death, at least not in a healthy way. Instead, she felt guilty and despondent over how unhappy she and my father had been with one another. Genuine tears and a willingness to cry out to the Lord would have softened my mom's heart, but bitterness became her lasting refuge. This situation was compounded when she learned that the cancer she had been fighting for years had migrated to her liver. Her doctors considered her time short. They recommended chemotherapy but weren't particularly hopeful. The drugs worked, however, and my mother's cancer entered a state of remission.

After her miraculous recovery, she was incapable of making the most of her second chance. Unfinished grief over my dad's passing kept her from capitalizing on life. Instead, she turned toward silent succor in the creature comforts of this world for survival. The grace that God had so lovingly poured out upon her was forgotten. The gratuitous appealed to my mom more than the Lord's favor. She decided that her continued existence on this earth was only going to be worth the effort if she could be certain booze was still a part of her life. It had helped her and my dad put up with each other for years. Now, it promised to anesthetize the pain of facing life without him.

My mom began camping out in the privacy of her little apartment with a large glass of vodka and orange juice always in hand. She seldom stepped outdoors. Thinking about the past kept her mind off other things. Any mention of Jesus made her want to change the subject.

Her physicians insisted that her two-pack-a-day nicotine habit and love affair with alcohol were going to kill her, even if the cancer remained in remission. She wouldn't listen. Every time her drinking and smoking came up, she became defensive and talked about the uselessness of "leading a horse to water." When I approached her with the thought that going to church might be good for her, she called the idea silly. She had decided that life's goodies were enough for her. Greater—or longer lasting—rewards weren't of interest; waiting for them meant she would have to explore the emptiness inside her soul, and there was too much pain there.

BROKENNESS 101

Grief work awaited my mother, along with the Savior's open arms, but she never got around to releasing her pain to him. He remained a distant acquaintance to her, instead of her best friend. She couldn't grasp the notion that winning means losing, or that God's grace is going to be made sufficient the minute we decide to fall upon the Rock that is Christ Jesus. Remember, Jesus told us that we must fall on him, or we will get crushed under the weight of self-effort and the utter ridiculousness of life.

Like Samson, my mother figured she could face her pain and loneliness all by herself, with no questions asked. She didn't have time to think about how Jesus might be able to fill the void left by my father's suicide. Her own agenda seemed to be working for now, and cancer was no longer frightening her into any vain promises about trying to be better—tomorrow. Ultimately, this attitude cost my mom her joy as well as her life.

My pastor, Chuck Smith, Jr., once spoke about such things. He wisely shared that the Lord introduces us to his holy curriculum by allowing life to be exasperating. It causes us to reflect on our need for a Savior in the first place. One class in particular—Brokenness 101—is meant to teach us a corollary lesson about learning how to give in. Withdrawing from the class or taking an "Incomplete" gets us nowhere. We have to pass this course to get the spiritual maturity degree we seek.

My mom wanted to be in control of her destiny without having to admit that she was a horribly lost soul. Jesus wanted to be first in her life in order to give her existence some meaning, but that would have required her to admit her life wasn't working in the first place. In addition, such a confession would have meant giving up a very old friend.

Booze had been around to comfort my mom a long time, while Jesus seemed much less tangible. So, she kept Jesus at a safe distance. This included avoiding going to church (which sounded "boring") and never bothering to read God's Word. Watching her daytime soap operas was much more to her liking.

How can any of us be so stubborn? I believe it's due to fear. We are afraid that if we don't grab the spoils that are immediately available to us, we will go without. In the end, we will be left empty-handed.

MAKING LIFE WORTH LIVING

The only way of making life worth living—and gaining the reward of God's eternal benevolence—is to let Jesus become Lord of our lives. This is the very thing he has wanted to do from the beginning of our walk with him. Jesus helps us set priorities for life that make the most sense. By making him our whole life, we discover what it means to make healthy choices and be free of the destruction that otherwise awaits us.

The surest way of accomplishing this task is to pray as often as possible. Through prayer, Jesus enters into every aspect of our lives as he becomes acquainted with our hearts. God's grace is made immediate as we learn that falling upon the Rock means calling upon the name of Jesus.

Prayer is a primary means by which the Lord Jesus Christ is made central in our lives. We are to pray to the Father in Jesus' name, recognizing that it is Jesus who bridges the gap between heaven and earth. Jesus told his followers that, upon his ascension into heaven, they could ask for anything in his name, so that their joy would be full (John 16:24). Jesus also taught his disciples how to pray, reminding them that the Lord was the only one who could meet all their needs—forgiving their sins, helping them avoid temptation, delivering them from evil, and ensuring they would see the kingdom of God come into existence (Matt. 6:10).

We have no excuses for not praying, even if we are at a loss for words. In fact, we are invited to let the Holy Spirit show us how to pray by simply giving voice to the innermost groaning of our hearts (Rom. 8:26). If we're confused about what prayer is all about, we simply need to practice doing it. Forget trying to employ lofty words. Prayer is supposed to be heart-to-heart conversation with the Lord by which we enter another reality—one which lifts us out of the pressing circumstances of our lives and into the thought that all things are possible through Christ who strengthens us.

REFUSING TO LEAVE THE GRAVE

My mom lost heart with my father's passing. Cancer had fled from her mortal body, but not dejection. She missed my dad and could only ruminate over how things might have been. By way of her morbid thought life, she was sowing to the flesh, obsessing over the past. Symbolically, this left her stuck at my father's grave, unwilling to move on with life. Melancholy became her spirit's guide.

When her cancer returned, Mom welcomed it. It gave the loneliness inside her soul a name. And it gave her threadbare life a new focus. Her days were suddenly marked off by frequent visits to the doctor's office and trips to the drugstore across the street. There she picked up her prescriptions, along with half-gallon bottles of Smirnoff's.

I do not mean to insinuate that if my mother had given her life to the Lord, all would have been well with her. I doubt the cancer would have disappeared a second time. What I am saying is that had she begun to call out to Jesus, renewal would have poured out to her and fulfillment would not have escaped her. There would have been a newfound hope for her by which light and truth would have entered her soul. Her days would have counted for something.

IT'S NEVER TOO LATE

One last thing must be understood about the significance of prayer. It's never too late to experience the grace of God. It's ours upon request. The Lord is always ready to pour out his unmerited favor, like living water into our thirsty souls. My mom found this out in the eleventh hour of her life. She finally admitted her need for Jesus and let me lead her in the "Sinner's Prayer." From that point on, her focus changed.

She no longer ruminated about the past. Her cancer didn't scare her anymore, and she began to laugh at how laughable life truly was. She also learned to cry over the losses in her life she had never acknowledged before. Most importantly, she discovered a desire to search God's Word, even sharing meaningful Scriptures with me in some of our last telephone conversations with each other.

Jesus' presence in her life made the difference. Three months later she died while I sang "Jesus loves you, this I know," gently holding her in my arms. God's grace was poured out in that moment, and Satan's hope that he could take my mother with him into eternal darkness was pulverized—center ring. Upon her victory over spiritual death, I imagined her being ushered into God's throne room by a legion of angels who wanted her to sit on her heavenly Father's lap. I am convinced that she sits there to this day, telling the Lord that it was all worth it.

UNEXPRESSED SADNESS

God's grace or the gratuitous—the decision is ours. Our fears over not getting anything out of the deal life has to offer can be combated, but only when we make prayer the primary vehicle by which our inherent need for God's grace is openly communicated. In response to our willingness to expose our hearts to him, God's peace, joy, and comfort are made immediately available to us.

I discovered this when I started suffering panic attacks six months after my mother's death. I had never experienced anything like panic in my life, so I didn't know what to think when it burst on the scene. My breathing suddenly became labored as a band of tension gripped my chest. Frighteningly, my heart raced, skipping beats. My vision was strangely altered, as though I were looking down a tunnel.

The first time the panic struck, I was driving on an expressway. After pulling off the road, I drove to a telephone booth, certain that a 911 call was the only thing that was going to save me. And, just as quickly as the attack began, it disappeared. Consequently, no call was made. I decided I wasn't dying after all and ascribed my suddenly departing symptoms to fatigue, worry, or an approaching flu bug. However, when the panic returned a few days later, I knew something was dreadfully wrong.

I figured I should schedule an appointment with a cardiologist. But one last source of a cure crossed my mind—praying to the Lord. I was back in my car when I decided to ask God to show me what was wrong. The answer I got was immediate, but made no sense to me. What I heard in my spirit was simply this: "You have never fully grieved your mother's death." I had never connected my racing heart with the unfinished grief work in my heart, yet the Lord was telling me that the two were intertwined. Shortly after receiving this answer, I again prayed. This time I asked the Lord to show me how to grieve the loss of my mom. What followed was an emotional season of soul-searching and God's grace being applied to a broken heart.

Memories of the times I felt closest to my mom soon surfaced, and I talked to the Lord about how much I missed her. Tears were almost immediate. Sometimes anger surfaced as well, and I heard God encouraging me to get it out while driving in my car. This was usually when I remembered how much I had felt cheated by Mom's passing. Pounding on the empty passenger seat beside me offered some relief.

Interestingly, I felt led to picture Jesus sitting next to me while I talked about my relationship with my mother. His presence seemed essential for getting to the bottom of things. Generally, the Lord would place Scriptures in my heart after one of our therapy sessions. These words of encouragement definitely brought healing to my wounded soul. One such passage reminded me that the Lord is a Father to the fatherless or motherless (Ps. 68:5). Once this thought was communicated to my spirit, I became acutely aware of the Lord's desire to be my Abba Father. I was more than ready to accept his offer.

My panic gave way to grief and I was finally able to cry in the heavenly Father's arms. My anxiety disappeared after that, and I finally felt I was going to make it—my heart wasn't going to fail after all.

SOULFUL PRAYER

Jesus told his followers, "Come to Me, all you who labor and are heavy laden, and I will give you rest" (Matt. 11:28). Rest comes in allowing Christ to show us how to be real with our pain; prayer is essential. He tells us to give up the pretense and learn how to become transparent with him. This requires we draw close enough to his Spirit to get to the real feelings inside.

We must learn how to pray from the bottom of our hearts if we are ever going to learn to be real with Jesus. Such prayer guarantees we will get to the heart of the matter when it comes to dealing with issues in our emotional lives. It also ensures that God's grace will be applied to those areas of our lives that need his holy ointment and gauze the most.

I have spelled out the word *prayer* as a way of showing what a soulful search of our hearts consists of and how it can be carried out successfully.

P = Praising the Father and remembering his many promises to his children (Quoting them can be helpful as a place to begin.)

R = Relating to Jesus as a friend and using normal speech in your conversations with him

A = Acknowledging your powerlessness while admitting your needs and telling God where it hurts

Y = Asking "Why?" Life can be very perplexing and our frustration must be expressed.

E = Expressing our thanks to God for his responsiveness

R = Resting in the Lord by letting his peace come upon us

Each step is important in learning how to pray. For instance, praising God helps us see that we can choose to "be anxious for nothing" while entering into prayer (Phil. 4:6). It causes us to see that worry involves a choice and that God is ready to respond to our decision to believe, that he wants to answer us. Remembering God's promises helps us see that every problem has a solution. Often, that solution is a single Bible verse we can quote to ourselves. A timely Scripture can bring sweet comfort, tiding us over while we wait for the Lord's plan to unfold in our lives.

Acknowledging our powerlessness and discomfort is essential to a healthy prayer life. We are compelled to see that our solutions aren't working and we must look to Jesus for the answers. Placing our focus on him as a friend is helpful in this regard. Talking to a friend is much easier than trying to relate to an "unapproachable light" in some faraway part of the universe. Feelings of immediacy are essential for getting in touch with our emotions.

Next, the "Why?" question certainly needs to be voiced, especially if we're dealing with issues of loss in our emotional lives. Why has God allowed us to suffer? Why has the Lord given the enemy permission to torment us? These questions usually hold no answer, but we need to learn to express the discomfort behind their existence. Asking why is helpful because it gives voice to our anguish and allows the sense of our powerlessness to become real.

Expressing real feelings means allowing the hurt inside to work its way out. It can also entail getting angry at Jesus. The Lord isn't squeamish about such things. If you're not certain what you're really feeling, ask the Lord to show you. Pastor Jack Hayford has suggested that when we approach God in prayer, we must be bold enough to open our hearts completely, declare our frustrations without hesitation, let the fullness of our pain be laid in his presence, and, whatever the anger, disappointment, or struggle, let our whole life be placed in his hands.

Finally, expressing our gratitude and resting in the Lord means allowing his peace to enter our minds. It might help to picture him holding you. It also can help to get the assistance of a trusted friend as you search for the grief inside. Talking to a pastor, counselor, or psychologist will give a person the opportunity to get some important things off his chest and provide the arms that may be needed.

ROADBLOCKS TO PRAYER

We must also be aware of things that will block an effective prayer life. It won't do us much good to lift holy petitions to the Lord if they're getting no higher than the ceiling. What might we be doing wrong that would cause the Holy Spirit to hang up on us after we've put in a call to him? Some of the following barriers should be considered.

1. Disobedience. Why should God give us his ear if we have chosen to plug ours to his commandments and his leading (1 Sam. 14:24-37)?

2. Secret sin. Why should God offer a helping hand if we're holding one of ours behind our back, clutching sin (Ps. 66:18)?

3. Stubbornness. Why should God give in to us while we are refusing to give in to him (Zech. 7:12-13)?

4. Self-indulgence. Why should God pour out his favor if we have decided to keep all of it for ourselves (James 4:3)?

5. Mistrust. Why should God answer prayer if we continue to mistrust him and remain doubting Thomases (James 1:6-7)?

Having considered such things, it might prove helpful to run through a mental checklist that helps us see where our focus needs to be in our prayer life.

- Focus on the Lord's graciousness, not on our badness. Any sins which need to be confessed can be carried to the foot of the Cross with the expectation that they will be immediately taken from our shoulders (Ezek. 36:25).

- Focus on what we are genuinely feeling and not on the form or style of the prayer. The Lord doesn't need us to spiritualize our emotions away by acting holy when we're feeling otherwise. He wants us to practice honesty with him (Matt. 6:5-8).

- Focus on God's Word rather than mindless chatter, so we are able to repeat promises relevant to our circumstances. In this way, we can offer reassurance to our own spirits that God is already at work in us figuring out a solution (Isa. 65:24).

- Focus on God's will, not our own agenda. We must accept God's timing and learn to rest in the knowledge that he never says "Oops!" (Eph. 1:9-10).

- Focus on what is currently happening in our lives. We must learn to go to the Lord in prayer whenever we are frustrated, angry, hurt, or dejected. Waiting only drives us into silence and the enemy's arms (John 10:10).

- Focus on God's faithfulness, not on how awful things look right now. We must not give up on the Lord; his plan will prevail (Lam. 3:22-24).

- Focus on the One to whom we are praying. It is the person of Jesus Christ, in whom all of God's promises are "yes" (2 Cor.

1:20). We are to pray in his name, claim his name over every situation we face, and acknowledge there is no other name given to men by which we may be saved (Acts 4:12).

■ Focus on giving thanks—by learning to be thankful in every situation. This becomes our way of spitting in the enemy's face. It is the spiritual gesture that guarantees we come out the victors after the bell has sounded (Col. 3:15).

To avoid the Samson trap, we must remember that we can't just gut it out. Faith is learning to talk to God while appropriating his grace and forsaking the gratuitous. A fruitful, constant prayer life makes us rich with the spiritual rewards of God's choosing.

THINGS TO THINK ABOUT AND DO

1. Keep a prayer journal. Make entries every day, writing out your thoughts to the Lord and expressing your innermost concerns. Ask him for his mercy and grace and keep track of what his responses are. Go back to some of your prayer requests a month or two after you have recorded them and see how faithful God has been.
2. Practice talking to Jesus conversationally. Speak to him as though he were sitting next to you, and try being candid with him. Talking aloud can be helpful. Also, practice memorizing some Bible verses by which God's promises for healing, support, nurture, or protection are made real for you. Try repeating these verses in your prayer time with the Lord.
3. If there is unfinished grief work in your life, now is the time to finish it. Is there someone you miss greatly? Write about your sadness.

    Sometimes grief can be hidden in any number of hazy symptoms. A deep sense of loss may be responsible for some of the following: You feel anxious much of the time; you feel alone; you feel listless or apathetic; you feel angry because disappointment seems inevitable; or, you are fearful that people close to you are bound to leave you. Find a counselor or friend with whom you can talk out these feelings.

12

BREAKING OUT
OF THE TRAP

Remember our point of departure in the journey toward a new identity in Christ? It was Point A and the fear we wanted to leave behind. Our final destination is Point B and the faith by which God intends to liberate our souls from our old way of doing business in this world. In making the trek, we become the new creation God has chosen to unveil to a dying world. Fear and faith stand in opposition to one another and represent the two realities that we contend with in reaching spiritual maturity. The first is born of our old nature and tells us to trust no one. The second is delivered to our hearts by the Holy Spirit upon our conversion in Christ. It tells us to trust in the Lord our God and live by his promises.

Once our sin has been removed, it is fear that stands between us and the faith the Lord wishes to release into our spirits. This is one reason why Jesus came into this world. He wanted to show us the path back to the truth of who we were created to be and how we were to function. God's original purpose in breathing life into a lump of clay was to give humanity the opportunity to worship him and enjoy his fellowship. Faith allows us to see God's plan for our existence established once more.

In Christ, we learn that fear no longer has any power over us as God's children. Faith in Jesus guarantees that we are set free from all the things that would otherwise frighten us, including our sin nature and death itself. Neither controls our destiny any longer. Jesus made this known when he said he was "the way, the truth, and the life" (John 14:6). He knew there was no other way back to God's truth unless we made him Lord of our lives. Through compliance to God's ordinances for our lives, faith grows within our hearts as we become mindful that Jesus' Spirit is making it all happen—just as he promised.

"HERE'S SAMSON!"

Samson chose to live in open rebellion to God. A living faith never became a reality to this wayward child because he never deferred to God's council. As a consequence, he lost his way in his journey between fear and faith and never found Point B. His Savior remained on the doorstep of his heart waiting for an invitation that never came. Meanwhile, Samson became a kind of spiritual outlaw who figured he could get himself to glory.

His inner man told him that as long as he had the attention of another beautiful woman, he didn't have to worry about seeking God's help. Beyond this, he continued putting on his gunslinger routine. The public eye still enthralled him, and he remained the fastest draw around.

But time was running out for Samson. As someone who stood outside the laws of God, his season of reaping was at hand. Samson fell for a Philistine woman named Delilah. Emotionally, he was a goner and so too was his anointing (Judg. 16:20). Satan was behind the whole thing, of course, and his agenda was made known to Delilah through her kinsmen: "And the lords of the Philistines came up to her and said to her, 'Entice him, and find out where his great strength lies, and by what means we may overpower him, that we may bind him to afflict him; and every one of us will give you eleven hundred pieces of silver' " (Judg. 16:5). Sin's ultimate reward may feel like cash in our pockets, but its desire is to afflict us. If given half a chance, darkness will do just that and grant us no mercy.

Delilah was Samson's siren, calling him to her bed and getting him to share his deepest secrets with her (Judg. 16:6). This sad tale causes us to see that boundaries need to be built around our words. If we become reckless with them or begin to reflect spiritual insincerity, we will be handing darkness one last advantage over us. Our witness will then be lost forever. Righteousness simply can't share the sheets with the devil without dire consequences. Jesus warned all believers: "Do not give what is holy to the dogs; nor cast your pearls before swine, lest they trample them under their feet, and turn and tear you in pieces" (Matt. 7:6).

WORDS COUNT FOR EVERYTHING

Samson paid little attention to what he was saying or to whom he was saying it. He made up his own rules, never realizing that words count for everything, because what comes out of our mouths measures the sincerity of our hearts (see Matt. 12:34). Hurtful words can pierce like a knife "but the tongue of the wise promotes health," says Proverbs 12:18. Scripture also tells us that salvation results from the confession of our lips (Rom. 10:10). Words bring life or death depending on what they encompass—love or acrimony; faith or denunciation. They tell the enemy what's going on in our hearts. Thus, the devil takes it upon himself to enter into the darkness of our souls when our words justify his efforts to overthrow our insincere spirits.

One afternoon at the hospital where I worked, another counselor and I were sitting in the nurse's station, killing time by joking with each other about our various personal health fears. I admitted that due to my wish to be sexually active until I was ninety, I was convinced that a fitting end to my days on earth would be prostate cancer. My fellow therapist shared he was certain a heart attack would take his life because of his "type A" personality. Each of us was getting a good laugh out of seeing how ludicrous our fears were—as well as how morbid our thinking could be. We were pointing at death and laughing heartily. Unknown to us, our words were heard by an invisible enemy. He was intent on making our mockery an excuse for infiltrating our lives.

We can speed up our day of reckoning by living our lives frivolously. The truth is, we are God's workmanship—created in Christ's likeness—to carry out God's plans for our existence. If we choose to live our lives foolishly, or if we let our words reflect an attitude of ambivalence or disinterest, then death may come prematurely. This certainly is to the devil's liking; he is spared the trouble of trying to keep our faith small or our witness ineffectual.

During my reckless conversation, unfeeling words were tossed out like confetti. My friend and I were making light of horrible diseases and the pain of those who suffer them. No boundaries were placed around our conversation—or our hearts. God's Word says, "He who guards his mouth preserves his life, but he who opens wide his lips shall have destruction" (Prov. 13:3). The apostle Paul warned all believers of the need to pay attention to what they were doing and saying, "for in doing this you will save both yourself and those who hear you" (1 Tim. 4:16). The point is, the devil will use our words against us. This is especially the case when our words suggest our fearful state is not to be taken seriously.

NEVER BEING MOVED

Within two weeks of our idle conversation about health, I found myself bent over in pain. I had awakened that morning realizing I wasn't going to be able to get myself out of bed. My wife assisted me as I tried standing up. My back was torturing me while I hobbled around thinking I must have pulled a muscle. This awkward situation continued for several days until I realized my back was becoming noticeably worse.

Slowly, my back started curving, as though I were developing some kind of crippling disease. A trip to the doctor seemed called for. Following some lab tests and a rather painful exam of my backside, I was shocked to find out I had severe prostatitis. My doctor told me I needed to be on a healthy dosage of antibiotics. This news was hard to believe. I had never had this problem in my life and now it was causing me to take on the likeness of a human pretzel.

In utter disbelief, I remembered joking around about my prostate; now I was suffering for it. The connection seemed obvious. The enemy had seen my insincerity concerning my health as license for a spiritual assault.

I learned that truth can never be taken lightly. The truth can be used against us when we approach it recklessly or fail to put boundaries around what we discuss. On the other hand, the Bible tells us that the person who walks uprightly, works righteousness, and speaks the truth in his heart will never be moved (Ps. 15:2, 5). Our spirit needs to be evaluated, its true intent understood. We have to compare its authenticity with what the enemy is likely to do with our verbal and spiritual "throwaways."

After leaving the doctor's office, I went home and prayed. I asked God's forgiveness for my indifference to human suffering. The very next day, I asked my colleague to pray with me while we asked for forgiveness from one another. Upon hearing my story, he was more than ready.

Within twenty-four hours of our mutual prayer, my back pain was gone and my curved spine began straightening itself. With prayer and spiritual cleansing, my spirit was transformed and my body was granted relief from the assault. Some will insist my improvement was merely the result of the medication prescribed for me. I am convinced of something else: "The Lord is near to all who call upon Him, to all who call upon Him in truth" (Ps. 145:18).

SIN'S FOOTPRINTS

The apostle Peter warned us of the ultimate danger of bedding with sin, either by our actions or by our words. He admonished us to "be sober, be vigilant; because your adversary the devil walks about like a roaring lion, seeking whom he may devour. Resist him, steadfast in the faith, knowing that the same sufferings are experienced by your brotherhood in the world" (1 Pet. 5:8-9). In short, Satan wants to eat us alive.

Remaining faithful is the only way to win the battle against him. That means we must be able to recognize sin's mug shot when it interrupts our walk with the Lord. I believe we'll know something is dreadfully wrong when:

- We aren't able to govern properly—ourselves or anyone else. We won't be able to get a handle on our lives and our positions of authority will start to suffer (see 1 Kings 3:9).

- We aren't able to understand the truths of the Bible or make sense out of what our pastor has been trying to teach us from the pulpit (see 1 Cor. 2:14).

- We don't know where we are going in life and feel horribly lost much of the time. Impulse or sentiment will seem to suffice rather than the certainty of the Lord's still, small voice (see Eccles. 2:14).

- We aren't able to judge the seasons of our lives. Our timing will always seem off, in terms of capitalizing on opportunities or moving on. We'll feel stuck (see Luke 12:56).

- We don't have a desire to know his Word or seek out his truths. Hunger for the things of God is diminished (see Ps. 92:5-6).

- We aren't able to receive constructive criticism (see Prov. 17:10).

- We aren't able to learn from our mistakes and grow (see Isa. 6: 9-10).

- We aren't capable of ruling our tongues, which continue to get us into trouble (see James 3:1-12).

SEEING THE OBVIOUS

When these symptoms become apparent in our lives, we need to do something—and quick. A good friend of mine, "Andrew," found this out too late. Some time ago he told me the Lord wanted him to expand his business. It was already a sprawling corporation, so further growth seemed hard to figure. But my friend was a visionary and a shrewd business man. His decisions about such things were always on target. Consequently, his plans went unchallenged.

Andrew insisted the Lord wanted him to turn his local business into a global one. And he was certain God's words to his spirit were meant to be reassuring. Sadly, Andrew discounted the messages his own family gave him regarding their life in the fast lane. His family was in constant turmoil. Things obviously were not going well at home, but Andrew didn't want to look in that direction. His future was "out there," where his business was leading him.

Andrew became a type of spiritual outlaw, just like Samson. God's will and purpose for his life (defined by his holy ordinances) were conveniently disregarded while Andrew became his own lawmaker. As a result, his wife became an emotional wreck whose condition steadily worsened. I observed her during their many get-togethers with his friends and associates, while she played hostess to the entourage. She always smiled and appeared friendly, but I could tell she was miserable inside. There was a sadness to her eyes that couldn't be hidden.

Meanwhile, Andrew admitted that when his wife was home alone, she quickly became depressed, isolating herself. She often spent the day in bed, saying she didn't have the energy to get out. He couldn't understand her lethargy and simply got angry at her for not being more involved at the club. There, he hoped she would exercise to get rid of the extra fifty pounds that bugged him so much.

If Andrew had bothered to ask his wife what was wrong, she probably would have shared her own timely words with him: she was dying of loneliness. But he couldn't (or wouldn't) hear this message. All the while, Andrew's older son also was trying to tell him something through his frequent encounters with the police. Previous charges of petty thievery had evolved into an arrest for auto theft, and jail time seemed certain. Yet all of this slipped the attention of a father bent on seeing his business do well.

Unswervingly, my friend continued to approach his corporate ventures with alarming zest. At home, no phone call went unanswered, and the fax machine was always waiting for his next transmittal. Family time got lost in frenetic ninety-hour work weeks. Still, Andrew insisted that keeping the business going right now would mean rich dividends for the family later.

My friend's addiction to work surely would have benefited from a twelve-step program of some kind. His underlying fears of devaluation and loss were obvious. They obviously fueled a pervasive need for overachievement. Nevertheless, Andrew had a bigger problem. He had lost sight of his true self and what being a loving human being looked like. Instead, a false self-image was erected in its place. That false self was seemingly intent on destroying everything around him.

JUDGING THE TIMES

If we give in to the Samson trap, we will become liars. We will decide that truth should be kept out of sight, while denying problems and their consequences. Such fallacies are common for all of us Samsons. We want the world to believe that everything is okay.

Bad times are invariably going to land in our laps, if we let the Samson in us do the talking. We won't see a thing until it's too late because pride will suggest nothing has to change: "Everything's fine!" Our worlds can be crumbling down all around us, and our false impressions will still give us something to smile about.

To combat this sickening tendency, we must learn to honestly face what our inner spirits are subtly telling us about our moral fiber. Admittedly, this is a struggle. Jesus once declared, "You know how to discern the face of the sky, but you cannot discern the signs of the times" (Matt. 16:3). He was indicting all of us for not being able to see the truth of our own hearts and what our lives are going to net for us.

Andrew's false sense of security got in the way of his seeing the obvious. His family's needs went undetected. He refused to look inward toward a heart growing cold, or outward toward a sky turning black. Ultimately, Andrew's wife ended up in a psychiatric treatment center for severe depression. Upon her release, she declared the marriage between them was over. Meanwhile, his son ended up serving eighteen months in jail, swearing he would never speak to his father again.

Most shocking of all, however, was the sudden downturn in my friend's business. Everything went sour, and he lost all of his major accounts within about three months. Andrew's lasting heritage to the corporate world was the news that he was declaring bankruptcy as his house went into foreclosure.

THE WAY OF PARADOX

God's desire is for that redeemed person we are becoming in Christ to come to center stage and start operating according to the divine principles meant to set us free. Otherwise, the storms of life will simply overtake us and leave us emotionally, financially, or spiritually ruined.

Jesus told us what has to be done to gain the personhood we seek in our walk of faith. He insisted that we needed to become his disciples, deny ourselves, and follow him. The old man needs to be left behind, while the new man (the one appointed to be holy and sanctified) commits to following Jesus.

This is really a matter of facing the spiritual truths set down for us in the Word of God and trying our best to live in obedience to them. The tough part is that while Jesus' invitation to follow sounds relatively easy, doing it is extremely difficult. The false self doesn't move out of the way that easily. Thankfully, the Lord is ready to lend a hand. His Holy Spirit lives to empower us to carry out the Father's will. If our hearts are turned toward pleasing him, the Holy Spirit is ready to help us achieve the victory we seek. All we need to do is get in step behind Jesus. This means living in accordance with his gospel rather than scratching our heads and trying to think things out. By the time we have come to some brilliant conclusion, Jesus will be in the next county and we'll be lost.

The simplest way to get in step with Jesus is to deny what the old man expects us to do and run the other way. A godly principle called *paradox* can help bring lasting change. Paradox involves doing the exact opposite of what we would otherwise consider doing. Paradox gets us to turn around and face reality and the new man's appointed destiny. We must be taught that letting go of something means holding on; holding on means letting go. God promises to give us the very thing we want—the moment we let go of it first. The instant we turn around and look the other way (taking our eyes off the object of our interest) we suddenly see the Father pushing it back out in front of us for the taking.

Jesus once told a man of great wealth who wanted to be his disciple to sell everything he owned and then come follow him (Mark 10:21). Another time, Jesus told his audience that whoever wanted to be great among his brothers would need to be a servant of all (Matt. 20:26). You get the idea. God's means of showing us the way to a life of faith is to spin us around a few times and head us in the other direction.

THINKING IN OPPOSITES

Thinking or behaving in opposites is a sure way of keeping the outlaw in each of us silent. If we feel like saying something when we're angry, saying nothing probably makes more sense. If we assume that we *must* do something to make things work out, doing nothing may accomplish more in the long run. Doing the opposite of what our flesh is recommending will undoubtedly give the new man a chance to speak on behalf of the Holy Spirit. Want to be in control? Try giving up control. Want to be strong? Try being weak. Want to get ahead? Step to the end of the line. Somehow, God turns it all around and makes things work out—but only after we head the other way.

To find the living faith we seek, we don't have to know what's wrong with our inner child, we just have to do a 180-degree turn and follow Jesus. This is the surest way to Point B. Looking back at the Samson Test may help.

The "old man" profile as identified by the test reflected a fearful response to what we genuinely hunger for spiritually. Items 1-30 reflected how falsehood has been erected to cover up our real spiritual needs. Such falsehood blocks the development of the "new man" character. In the list below, items from the test are identified according to what our heart is truly seeking, and how the quest of the new man can be realized through an opposite response.

Refer back to your test answers on pages 50-51. Take each item you answered "True" and look here at its paradoxical response. For instance, if you answered true to item 3 on the Samson Test, go to the third item below and try the opposing response. In the process, we "put off" the old nature by "putting on" the new. Fear is exchanged for faith as we truly become new creatures in Christ.

Counterfeit Needs of the Old Man	Paradoxical Response of the New Man
1. To look good	Try looking the way you feel or deliberately "dressing down."
2. To hide one's shortcomings	Tell someone what embarrasses you about yourself.
3. To avoid disapproval	Ask someone to tell you about something they dislike about you.
4. To be self-critical	Accept others' compliments. At the end of the day thank the Lord for what you've heard.

Counterfeit Needs of the Old Man	Paradoxical Response of the New Man
5. To gain attention	Tell your audience what you're doing and then ask someone for a hug instead.
6. To be perfect	Ask someone for constructive criticism.
7. To always want more	Admit your problem and join a suitable twelve-step program.
8. To make fun a false god	Try taking the focus off the good time you're having and put it on whether others are having fun. Do things they want to do.
9. To insulate ourselves	Don't use other people to keep yourself "up." Instead, choose to be alone and listen to some classical music.
10. To do things in excess	Give up partying for a while and spend the next four Saturday nights at a local church.
11. To have your needs met	Practice meeting someone else's needs.
12. To be compulsive	Try fasting the one thing you can't live without.
13. To get even	Forgive someone who hurt you and do something kind for them.
14. To be in control.	Pick a situation in which control seems paramount and do nothing. Let someone else know you want them to be in control for awhile.
15. To always be confident/strong	Tell someone you need help.
16. To never be "down"	Share your sadness with someone.
17. To always be the winner	Practice losing and being happy for the "other guy."
18. To be dominating	Practice being quiet and listening when you differ with someone.
19. To never be alone	Practice being alone and spend time with the Lord in prayer.

Counterfeit Needs of the Old Man	Paradoxical Response of the New Man
20. To have proof of love.........	Do something loving daily for someone else.
21. To distract oneself............	Try doing nothing for an evening and reflect on what it felt like by writing about it afterward.
22. To be sexual	Join a men's group and learn to share feelings with others.
23. To "feel" God	Join a Bible study and learn about who God truly is.
24. To avoid looking inward.......	List three habits you want to be rid of, and seek help.
25. To make love a contest........	Confess that you're being selfish and do something nice for your partner.
26. To spend money to feel good ..	Go to a thrift store, find an item to purchase, and wear it.
27. To keep score	Throw away the score card and learn to give with a cheerful heart. Be the one who picks up the tab for a month.
28. To receive praise	Give gifts in secret.
29. To get something in return.....	Share your real motive in giving and ask forgiveness.
30. To always want something else ..	Take the gifts you receive for six months and give them to a charity. Begin tithing on a regular basis; volunteer time.

The willingness we show to do the opposite of what seems so natural to us will determine our success at becoming new in Christ. If we approach our lives in the context of the principle of paradox, we will begin to see real change in our hearts. What is required is a willingness to pick up the cross of obedience while laying down the one marked "My Way." I pray that we all can break out of the trap of self and become true disciples of Jesus, no matter what direction he's heading.

THINGS TO THINK ABOUT AND DO

1. Outline those things you talk about or words you speak that you know are dangerous to you. Take this list to the Lord in prayer and ask him to teach you how to guard your tongue against the evil that would use these words against you.

2. We may be "spiritual outlaws" like Samson, disregarding God's laws and living by our own. If so, our thinking will give our hearts away. The following list notes some attitudes that spiritual outlaws might have. It has been especially helpful for the inmates I work with. Recognizing these attitudes in our own lives can highlight our inner insincerities and lead to repentance.

SPIRITUAL OUTLAWS OFTEN:

DEMONSTRATE ONE-OF-A-KIND THINKING
- They feel different and better than others.
- They have unrealistic expectations.
- They quit at the first sign of failure.

ARE CARELESS WITH RESPONSIBILITY
- They find responsibility boring and unsatisfying.
- They have no sense of obligation.

SEE THEMSELVES AS GOOD, EVEN BETTER THAN OTHERS
- They focus on positives.
- They don't acknowledge destructive behavior.

ACT LIKE VICTIMS
- They avoid accountability.
- They avoid punishment.
- They keep the focus on others.

SHOW EXTREME IMPATIENCE

- They want everything right now.
- They don't learn from the past.
- They don't use the present to plan for the future.

DEMONSTRATE CLOSED THINKING

- They are secretive.
- They are closed off from what others say.
- They are not self-critical.

ACT LIKE OTHER PEOPLE ARE PROPERTY

- They believe they own everything.
- They use people.
- They accept no authority except their own desires.

ATTEMPT TO ALWAYS BE IN CONTROL

- They manipulate.
- They are deceitful.
- They control others through anger.

GIVE UP WHEN THE GOING GETS TOUGH

- They avoid boring and unpleasant assignments.
- They say "I can't."
- They mean "I won't."

SAMSON'S GREATEST HOUR

A t last, Samson's wayward spirit caused him to bend under the weight of sin and fall tragically short of God's final destination for him. Capitalizing on Samson's weaknesses and Delilah's beauty, Satan brought about his plan of destruction for Samson's life. Samson confided in Delilah, telling her, "No razor has ever come upon my head, for I have been a Nazirite to God from my mother's womb. If I am shaven, then my strength will leave me, and I shall become weak, and be like any other man" (Judg. 16:17). Delilah was all ears. In no time, Samson was tied up and his manly mane was gone—along with his strength.

Samson was mistaken about what a call to holiness meant for a believer, and he ultimately paid a dear price. He had wrongly concluded that he was somehow exempt from the natural consequences of choosing sin over God's will—repeatedly. Meanwhile, he cheerfully faced his new situation, declaring, "I will go out as before, at other times, and shake myself free!" But as the Bible explains, "he did not know that the Lord had departed from him" (Judg. 16:20). He thought brute strength would pull him through once more. No more. Things were dramatically different now, and darkness was raising its hands in victory.

Samson was taken to a Gaza jailhouse to await his execution. He was blinded and tied to a millstone—around which he was forced to march, day in and day out. How humbling for someone who had never lost at anything before! Still, losing has many things to teach us, and the lessons can be very liberating.

"Look—I've Got Real Hair"

Remember the story of my own hair loss? Losing hair ultimately showed me that greatness comes by way of baldness and the blinding misfortunes of this world. In fact, being stripped of my manhood taught me what being a man was really all about. *It's about choosing to surrender our hearts to the Lord, knowing that any other plan is going to land us in mental prison.* Only God and his mercy can show us the way toward spiritual adulthood—and freedom.

Hair represented a source of strength to me. When I was in the army in the seventies, having real hair meant being courageous. My drill sergeant told me and my fellow "grunts" (or foot soldiers) that we had "real hair" if we could handle assignments that were perilous or required raw courage.

For men, hair certainly is a sign of virility—but only from the world's point of view. God's spin on the subject of hair is slightly different. In God's eyes, it isn't our appearance that makes us great, handsome, strong, or the guy who can do it all. Instead, holy attributes are what make us shine, and they are generally unseen by the naked eye. This is what having real hair is all about in God's army.

Gaining Our Spiritual Release

Something truly joyous was happening for Samson. He was inching toward freedom. Such release comes in the guise of a living faith erected in our souls as we learn to give up on ourselves and trust wholly in God. In this manner, a much-needed transformation takes place in our hearts. It is characterized by an exchange of our temporary encounters with the Holy Spirit for a more permanent relationship with the living God.

All of Samson's earlier demonstrations of spiritual power were the result of the Holy Spirit's dropping by and helping Samson out as needed. The Spirit simply came upon him and enabled him to do the incredible. These exhilarating moments reflected God's willingness to get Samson out of trouble as the Lord went to war against unrighteousness. However, Samson's heart was no different afterward. Image, power, satiation, sentiment, and the gratuities of this life continued to anesthetize him against life's jagged edges.

Thankfully, the harsh reality of his newest predicament caused his thinking to turn. Samson realized he needed something more enduring than a quick fix. God was ready to accommodate his change of heart. In fact, the Lord was waiting to invade Samson's life in a new way—one that would promote a sense of power through the permanent habitation of God's Holy Spirit.

THE SPIRIT'S MISSION

There are many things we need to know about the Holy Spirit, and we have a lifetime to learn what they are. One important fact is that the Holy Spirit is a person, one of three in the Holy Trinity. He also is the counterpart of Christ on this earth. Jesus told his disciples that they would not regret his leaving them after his ascension; his departure would guarantee the arrival of "another Counselor" (or Helper) who would be with them forever (John 14:16).

It's also important to know that the Holy Spirit carries out three distinct missions. First, he calls all people to repentance and everlasting life through a newfound belief in Jesus. In this context, the Spirit nags at us until we turn our hearts toward righteousness.

Second, the Holy Spirit is God's witness to the world, coming to people in order to empower them. Samson's story typifies this situation. It shows God is willing to give us a dose of his power when it pleases him and affords him some advantage in a given situation.

Third, the Holy Spirit dwells in the hearts of all true believers to fill them. For this reason, the Bible shows us the apostle Peter, on the day of Pentecost, telling all new converts in Jerusalem, "Repent, and let everyone of you be baptized in the name of Jesus

Christ for the remission of sins; and you shall receive the gift of the Holy Spirit" (Acts 2:38). Earlier, the disciples had noticed tongues of fire accompanying the Holy Spirit's visitation. Scripture tells us they were filled with the Holy Spirit and even began speaking in foreign languages, as a manifestation of the Spirit's presence in their lives (Acts 2:1-4).

To Live Is Christ

While the Holy Spirit resides within the hearts of all believers, functioning as a seal of God's approval, we don't always live out the kind of coexistence the Lord envisions for his children. Ideally, the Spirit would like to enter into a holy partnership with us, by which we might finally be liberated from the pull of darkness on our souls. His greatest desire is to be a heavenly power source compelling us to live a life of righteousness, so that the world we live in might be altered.

Such power awaits us when our thoughts turn from the temporal to the eternal. In that moment, the Holy Spirit fills our hearts with his power, or *dunamis*. This Greek word—translated as "mighty," "power," and "wonderful"—shares roots with the English word *dynamite*. Picture God placing a stick of dynamite under us by which we can finally bring the house down—spiritually speaking. It becomes an indwelling source of life-changing power when we decide God is all we want in our lives.

For Samson, the kind of spiritual overhaul I mean led to a rather unassuming result: "the hair of his head began to grow again after it had been shaven" (Judg. 16:22). God's idea of hair was taking the place of the world's version, and sin would finally be the loser. We read:

> When the people saw him, they praised their god; for they said: "Our god has delivered into our hands our enemy, the destroyer of our land, and the one who multiplied our dead." So it happened, when their hearts were merry, that they said,

"Call for Samson, that he may perform for us." So they called for Samson from the prison, and he performed for them. And they stationed him between the pillars. (Judg. 16:24-25)

God was working a real miracle in Samson's life. Samson no longer had to be the hero. Instead, he was content waiting on the Lord for further instruction, even if that meant bearing the world's derision. Now he was standing in the middle of a huge amphitheater, facing the mockery of thousands of Philistine loyalists. They wanted his blood, thinking that his God had abandoned him. The idol Dagon had seemingly won the day. Yet, for the first time, Samson decided to place his trust in the Lord rather than his brawn and see what the heavenly Father was going to do. In this spirit, Samson asked a young boy standing next to him to lend him a hand.

Imagine the irony of the moment as a once-heroic "tough guy" asked a little boy for help, but that is an index of God's grace in our lives. We too can ask for help while allowing God's strength to be perfected through our weaknesses. He whispered to the kid, "Let me feel the pillars which support the temple, so that I can lean on them" (Judg. 16:26). He was choosing to lean on God's provision (and invisible presence), as well as committing himself to the dying process.

WATCHING THE WORLD CAVE IN

Samson then prayed to the Lord and took hold. His prayer was a brief one. It reflected an emptying of his heart toward humility, so that he might finally be empowered with God's strength. In that moment, he was "filled" with the Spirit and made ready to bring the world down around him. With a new spirit—and a new head of hair to prove it—he pleaded for one last shot at the enemy. He stepped out in faith, rather than presumption, and that made all the difference (Judg. 16:28).

Samson had finally arrived at Point B. He was truly leaning on the Lord and not on his own muscles. He was reaching out with both arms while seeing nothing and recognizing the true essence of faith. There was no attempt to power-up one more time. Rather, he openly expressed the desires of his heart while admitting he deserved nothing in particular. He found his hope squarely in God.

> Samson took hold of the two middle pillars which supported the temple, and he braced himself against them, one on his right and the other on his left. Then Samson said, "Let me die with the Philistines!" And he pushed with all his might, and the temple fell on the lords and all the people who were in it. So the dead that he killed at his death were more than he had killed in his life. (Judg. 16:29-30)

In like manner, the Lord wants us to be able to take a stand for him. Temples must fall, so we may hear the sound of our flesh (and the old man) breathing its last. This is the only way to "attain to the resurrection" and become spiritually strong in the eyes of the Lord. It is also the only means of abating the soul's appetite for all it longs for. To accomplish these things, we have to be able to cross over from death to life, choosing death over life: "That I may know him and the power of his resurrection, and the fellowship of his sufferings, being conformed to his death, if, by any means, I may attain to the resurrection from the dead" (Phil. 3:10-11).

SAMSON'S CONTEMPORARY COUNTERPART

"Mike" was a respected counselor, author, and teacher whom I had been counseling for months. His problem was an obsessional interest in cross-dressing and covert exhibitionism. Whenever he found himself physically aroused, his thoughts turned toward dressing in women's lingerie and going somewhere to experience the danger of being found out. He hated himself for doing such things and had already lost a marriage to this behavior. All the while, his "public" never knew about Mike's private demons. He was admired by his clientele and sought after as a speaker in his community. Simply put, he was a twentieth-century Samson.

Mike and I spent many weeks looking into the issues of his past to see why these behaviors played themselves out in his life. However, we weren't making any progress, and Mike was heading out for a weekend in another state where he had been invited to appear on a local television station. The opportunity to plug his newest book meant he could shine publicly once more. He wasn't looking forward to the trip, though, because he was afraid he would again act out his dangerous compulsions. This thought left him feeling totally unsafe with himself.

Interestingly enough, I got a call from Mike immediately after his trip. He wanted to schedule an appointment right away and said he had some exciting news. Once in my office, he told me an incredible story.

Mike began by recounting how he had felt comforted by the thought that his speaking engagements and TV appearance were going to keep him pretty busy. The idea of being alone in his hotel room to think certain sexual thoughts frightened him; staying busy seemed essential. But before he left his room behind, he decided to glance at the program guide sitting on the TV. His heart leaped when he learned that adult movies were available through a special hookup via the front desk.

Just as suddenly, his spirit sank. He realized a spiritual battle was ahead, and he would probably lose. Mike's temporal, worldly side always seemed more persuasive than the Holy Spirit. Out of sheer frustration, he was convinced that giving in to his dark impulses was probably the easiest thing to do. This story is one I've heard many times over. Satan tells us we're losers and God can't possibly use us in his kingdom. Our fallible human spirit tells that teaching God's Word is far easier than living it. So, we hide away with our sordid lifestyles that seem untreatable, while hoping we can go on fooling the world into believing we are righteous men of God.

Even though Mike had been earnestly trying to get an upper hand on his sexual tendencies, nothing short of a miracle was going to help now. The TV called to him, and he was ready to heed that call. While pondering his forthcoming fall from grace, Mike looked in the mirror and saw a spiritual has-been staring back at him. He felt unqualified to be a teacher of God's holy Word or any kind of disciple to the lost souls of this world. He felt just as lost as they were. The apostle Paul spoke of the same frustration when he admitted that the things he wanted to do for the Lord were often left undone, while the things he hated to admit about himself were the things he did (see Rom. 7:15-20).

But Paul didn't let the topic drop at that point. He went on to admit that it was only through the presence of Jesus Christ in his life that this situation became tolerable for him. Otherwise, all was lost. The same was true for Mike. He needed to come to an understanding that he would always need Jesus to empower him.

BLINDED BY FEAR

Exhibitionism represented a core issue in Mike's life. It was the one behavior he continued to obsess over as a Christian, seeing it as something that deserved God's judgment. In truth, his countless moments of cross-dressing or silent exposure had simply elicited the Lord's mercy and grace. Nevertheless, whenever the impulse to do either arose, Mike felt fortunate to have escaped God's wrath yet one more time. He figured it was only a matter of time before the Lord's impatience caught up with him. Every time he fell, he felt ashamed that he had gotten no further in his Christian growth. Having to go to the Lord with an attitude of repentance seemed repugnant; he felt like the one untrainable kid in God's family.

After losing his skirmish with the flesh that night, Mike felt compelled to pray the next morning while showering. He had spent the previous night watching an X-rated film and parading around in women's lingerie with the curtains of his hotel room wide open. Now, he was listening to his cassette player in the bathroom. It carried the voice of Jack Hayford telling his audience the importance of engaging in a heavenly prayer language. Pastor Hayford's pointed out that speaking to the Lord through the gift of tongues allowed the Father to touch a part of us that would otherwise go untouched. He recommended that praying in tongues was a step toward intimacy with the God of this universe through whom inner healing was made available.

The idea seemed sensible and offered renewed hope to Mike's dying soul. He had never formally asked the Lord for this particular gift. In fact, Mike had never given much thought to any of the gifts of the Spirit. Still, the sermon Mike was hearing told him to hold on to his faith rather than give up. Jesus wanted to be his Holy Psychiatrist by baptizing him with fire.

THE SIGNIFICANCE OF A HEAVENLY LANGUAGE

What I am about to share remains a controversial subject among Christians. It has to do with how the Holy Spirit chooses to accommodate himself in our lives once he has come to live in our hearts. He wishes to bless us with gifts that represent the unique way God has of empowering each of us to serve the body of Christ (Rom. 12).

Speaking in tongues is one such gift the Holy Spirit will utilize, but there are many others. These may include prophecy, exhortation, teaching, giving, and so on. The bottom line is that God's Spirit decides how or in what manner to announce himself.

Our baptism in the Spirit entails a point of ignition to our human spirit by which planetary constraints are discarded and we begin to operate supernaturally. Two things are required to ensure the outcome: the Spirit's unction and a burning desire to finally give in to God completely.

As an example, when it comes to glossolalia (or speaking in tongues) we must suspend the need to keep things formal. We must be willing to give up our need to make sense of what we are saying or why. Instead, we must allow the Holy Spirit to form our words, trusting that he will provide understanding at a deeper level of our being. In essence, speaking in tongues is a statement of faith: it declares our words don't count anymore, while the words the Holy Spirit supplies will suffice in getting to the bottom line. Embarrassment can't be allowed to stand in the way of our desire to be swept off our feet by the Spirit's enraptured speech.

Today the church is divided on the subject of tongues, with some questioning the contemporary reality of the gift or its relative importance to the church. However, I think it is fair to say that speaking in tongues (as much as being "slain" in the Spirit, or any number of other manifestations of the Spirit) amounts to approaching our heavenly Father with reckless abandon. It encapsulates our desire to give up image altogether, while presuming God knows what the heart most hungers for: intimacy with the Lord. Such intimacy can provide the inner healing needed for our weary souls.

RELEASED BY GOD'S POWER

Mike was desperate for intimacy with God, but he felt ineligible for it; he kept returning to sinful thoughts and feelings. Now, in the privacy of the hotel room, Mike said he dropped to his knees right in the shower and asked the Lord for a deeper-level relationship as evidenced by a heavenly prayer language. He wanted to be able to speak in tongues in order to be released into the care of his heavenly Father in a new way. Human understanding and spiritual formulas hadn't brought the healing he sought or the freedom he needed from compulsions that shamed him.

An answer was immediate. He told me he heard the Holy Spirit's voice simply say, "Open your mouth and begin making sounds."

Mike's initial sounds were apparently awkward and silly. He felt the whole exercise was stupid. But something inside him said, "Keep going!" He reasoned that since receiving anything from the Lord is a gift of faith, he needed to trust God rather than waste time evaluating something he wasn't supposed to understand anyway. The sounds, meanwhile, began to take on a resonance. It seemed a language was forming inside Mike's spirit, despite his doubts and apprehensions. At the same time, images began forming in his mind: pictures of events that had occurred early in his life. He had always remembered these events, but had attached no importance to them. Now, the Holy Spirit was definitely directing his attention to them for reasons he couldn't fathom.

He saw himself as a child, standing in a bathroom with his mother. He remembered inadvertently seeing his mother undressing. Mike recalled being transfixed by her appearance. His mother's willingness to let him look a very long time had seemed wrong but inviting. Then, his mother's decision to let Mike touch her "there" made his heart swoon. The scene ended when Mike's mother told him to go and play while she finished dressing. He remembered turning and walking away, noticing a pair of his mother's underwear on the floor. They had become a lifelong reminder of the closeness he had achieved with his mother there in her bathroom.

Something very primitive and very wrong occurred in that moment of coming to know his mother. She had undoubtedly seen the incident as an act of innocence and childish curiosity. For Mike, however, the experience associated an emotional closeness to his mother with physical flesh and clothing. In that moment, his heart was bonded to darkness; love and shame were united in his thinking.

The wanton seemed mysteriously available and demanded satisfaction of deeper-level cravings—all of which was Mike's budding sin nature. Affection was now linked with shame and the longing for something forbidden. Once he had arrived at adulthood, all of this was symbolized by the undergarments Mike felt he needed to wear in order to feel the exhilaration he hungered for: the carnal nature's counterfeit for intimacy.

This psychological explanation came later in my office, but Mike's healing came immediately upon his asking in that shower stall. The memory of his mother brought him to tears. As he cried, he felt the comforting presence of the Holy Spirit. His new prayer language had paved the way for a release of deep pain. His time of heavenly communication with the Holy Spirit had brought knowledge, as well as a sense of purity and holiness Mike hadn't known before. Fittingly, the Lord chose a bathroom to bring that healing about, since it had also been a bathroom where Mike had experienced the wounding of his soul.

GETTING ANGRY AT FEAR

Throughout the next day Mike felt assured he had gained the victory over sin. He couldn't say why, but he sensed he was different, inside and out. He praised the Lord and thanked him for what he was certain would be a turning point in his life.

By evening, Mike was back in his hotel room anticipating a quiet night free of temptation. He had called the front desk that morning and requested the adult channels be disconnected in his room. Later that night, he was checking out the movies on TV when he realized that only one of the three adult channels had been disconnected. The struggle began, and after Mike acted out his sexual aberration yet another time, fear became his companion in the hotel room. He was sure God was fed up with his poor performance as a Christian. He went to bed completely dejected, imploring the Lord to show him what to do to win his battle over sin.

The next morning, he awoke feeling a new kind of peace hovering over him. First, he realized that joining a twelve-step support group was a must. I had been recommending it for weeks, but Mike hadn't been ready. Now he felt encouraged by the idea.

The other thing uppermost in his mind was that yesterday's defeats were meaningless. Today was brand new in the Lord. All of his many failures didn't seem important anymore. He saw his walk with the Lord boiling down to one fundamental question: Where did his safety come from? Was it tied to his continuing efforts to "get it right" while living in constant fear of forsaking God's Spirit? Or, was the Good News really meant to be good news—even for him?

In that instant Mike chose to stop obsessing over his sin nature. A wonderful thing happened. He stopped being afraid. He decided that by focusing on Christ's finished work on the cross, he could move away from self-hatred. All he had to do was push out any scornful thoughts that might arise with those that reflected a greater truth: Jesus is the answer to all of our problems, no matter how dark the hour. Mike did this by saying, "My badness doesn't matter. It has already been nailed to the Cross. It is God's goodness in me that permits me to face today. Yesterday doesn't exist any longer." Perhaps the apostle Paul said it best:

> And you, who once were alienated and enemies in your mind by wicked works, yet now He has reconciled in the body of His flesh through death, to present you holy, and blameless, and irreproachable in his sight—if indeed you continue in the faith, grounded and steadfast, and are not moved away from the hope of the gospel which you heard, which was preached to every creature under heaven, of which I, Paul, became a minister. (Col. 1:21-23)

Mike knew in his heart that he would no longer have to keep track of all those self-help formulas that showed him the way to recovery. Something better had presented itself to him: peace of mind. In that same instant, he decided to get angry at fear. He even rebuked its presence in Jesus' name.

SIN AND HEALING

God isn't put off by our sin. He is willing to apply his grace as needed. What he needs from us is honesty about our sin natures. We need to be able to go to him free of self-incrimination, acknowledging our helplessness over sin's tug on our hearts.

However, if we are approaching inner healing believing that we can deal with all the hurt inside and sin no more, we will be sorrowful creatures indeed. Sin and healing have nothing in common. Despite God's healing touch, we remain sinful in our hearts—no matter what. Healing doesn't guarantee that we'll be fine from now on. Sin remains a permanent condition of our souls that requires the Lord's continuing intervention. We need not be afraid of sin;

we just need to be smart enough to know what to do about it.

Fearing sin allows it to master us. Hating it is what we're called to do, but that requires us to see things God's way. Sin can only be defeated when we realize God is waiting to love us the moment we slip up. We can stop keeping count of how often we have blown it; God doesn't give up on us.

Healing of distant memories had been part of the answer for Mike. But experiencing the truth of what Jesus had done for all of us on the cross had been God's ultimate retort to the shameful person hiding inside Mike's heart. We need not fear that sin excludes us from God's company, no matter how often we fail. From our heavenly Father's point of view, we're perfect in Christ already. That truth has to work its way into our hearts in order for us to be set free from fear. Anguish doesn't belong in the soul of the believer—only the hope that *Abba,* our Daddy-God, is always ready to forgive and forget.

ASK AND YOU SHALL RECEIVE

Fear may be pushing you around right now. It will insist there are things you can do (besides facing sin) to feel better about yourself. Self-help books or endless hours in a therapist's office can become a side-step around the issue of your powerlessness against sin. However, sin's hold on you won't be eliminated through recovery.

Our insufficiency in facing sin has to be admitted. This means seeing God's plan for our salvation and making use of it through the confession of our sins. Repenting of our allegiance with darkness is necessary until real change begins to manifest in our hearts. After all, repeatedly asking for God's forgiveness is not only humbling, it also causes us to give up any plans for saving ourselves.

Next, comes the opportunity to see God manifest himself uniquely in our lives. This in turn requires that we give up any fears about looking silly. We must become wholehearted in asking God for power from on high—even to the point of looking ridiculous. This is the only way we are going to break the cords of our sin nature and find lasting joy in the Lord. For this reason, we need to carry out three simple steps.

1. Ask God for the filling of his Holy Spirit. This must include a burning desire to be done with any plans of our own for getting better. Instead, we must learn how to rely on God's way of doing business. We must wait upon him for a tongue of fire from above rather than resorting to self-promotion and charcoal briquettes. I believe one place to begin is in seeking a new prayer language. Speaking in tongues is one way of sharing our innermost feelings without worrying about how to get our point across.

2. Believe that, upon request, our desire to be empowered is granted. We receive God's Holy Spirit the same way we did our new birth in Christ—through faith. If our request seems to be getting us nowhere in particular, we should keep asking. Remember, God rewards those who diligently seek him. We should also keep in mind that such power is meant to be used to God's glory and not our nobility. He gets to choose the moment and the means by which any such gift will arrive on the scene.

3. Commit to a plan of making our gifts a reality by exposing ourselves to their manifestation and application. We must search the Scriptures as to the exact nature of God's gifts. The fourteenth chapter of 1 Corinthians is a good place to begin. Attending a seminar, talking with your pastor, or reading a book on the subject of spiritual gifts may also prove helpful. Mostly, we must be bold enough to express one of the gifts as we become aware of what it entails. A good rule of thumb is that our gift will typically benefit someone else, will be carried out in an unassuming manner, and will arrive when God decides his intervention is needed.

FILLING THE EMPTY PLACES

I believe that our faith expands through discovering what the baptism of the Holy Spirit represents to all believers: a filling of the empty places of our hearts through God's intimate involvement in our lives. It allows us to get past our many fears because God empowers us to do the impossible through a permanent sense of his divine presence. As a by-product, our he-man routine can be discarded while the Samson trap is resolved forever.

The origin of the word *baptize* will give us insights into what it is that God sets out to accomplish. In Greek, *baptizo* literally means "to dip" or "to wet completely." It was frequently used when referring to dyeing a garment.

When we get dropped by the hand of the Lord into the flames of a situation from which we cannot escape, we're definitely going to come out changed. The blackness of worldly influence will be boiled away and a whiteness born of purity and righteousness will take its place. That's what a living faith in Christ will do for us under God's watchful eye. We get dipped in order to dye—that is, *die*—to the things that have colored our lives.

This is what my hair problem ultimately meant for me. I wasn't going to escape the baptism of fire delivered to my darkened soul. My hair was gone for good, and it left behind the dreadful realization that I would be scarred for life. A hairpiece hid the outer scars, but inside I was still fighting with God over why this worst-case scenario had happened to me. His answer came in a most interesting way.

During one of my crazy moments, I tried to shake some magic from God by placing a Bible on top of my head. I hoped that a miraculous healing might result from something strictly superstitious. When I removed the Scriptures from my head, however, I discovered that a bloodstain from my scalp had imprinted itself on the open pages of my Bible. I read the verse covered by the stain, which said, "Trust in the Lord with all your heart, and lean not on your own understanding; in all your ways acknowledge Him, and He shall direct your paths. Do not be wise in your own eyes; fear the Lord and depart from evil. It will be health to your flesh, and strength to your bones" (Prov. 3:5-8).

I believe these verses were given to me to keep me moving in the right direction—toward Christ and the embodiment of lasting hope. To be healed of my shallow idealism, I needed to trust my

Savior. Only then would I be set free from fear and faithlessness.

My depressing ordeal brought me to my knees, where I asked God what he wanted me to do. He quietly told me to ask for the baptism of the Holy Spirit. Not knowing exactly what was in store, I obeyed. What followed was the sweetest moment I have ever experienced as a Christian. My heart felt fully at peace with the Lord, and I heard him say, "Now, feed my lambs." I knew in that moment that I would always be a person who wanted to make Christ the center of his life.

In addition, my heart swelled to know I would be allowed to serve God by ministering to his body. Suddenly, being a psychologist paled in comparison to knowing the risen Lord and experiencing the truly miraculous healing power of the Holy Spirit. That power was something God called on me to share with his children.

A Prison Yard, a Tree, and a Lone Path

The purpose of my writing this book can be summed up best through a dream I had some years ago. I've come to realize that the dream was the Lord's way of showing me the path toward spiritual freedom, the same one Samson traveled. In the dream, I stood on a platform above a large grassy area surrounded by walls. The walls were at least fifteen feet high, with no doors or windows. Meanwhile, in the center of this "prison yard" was a large tree with limbs that stretched in all directions, forming a canopy above the ground.

A single path led up to the tree in the center of the enclosure, and on the path was an old man in a wheelchair. He rolled slowly to the base of the tree and stood up. At the instant he arose, he stretched out his arms toward the tree and exclaimed in a loud voice, "I've been healed!" At this same moment, an angelic choir broke out in song, and thousands of voices joined in praise to the Lord. As I looked on, I immediately knew the lyrics of the song, though I had never heard it before. I began singing with the invisible host that surrounded me and felt utterly exhilarated. Then, the dream suddenly ended. The instant it did, the lyrics of the song were gone from my mind. Nevertheless, I was awake and in tears because of an overwhelming sense of awe.

Since I had the dream, interpretations have come and gone. One has stuck with me, however. I believe the Holy Spirit wanted to show me the very thing he needs to show all of us: Freedom comes in seeing our imprisonment to the circumstances of our lives and choosing to place our focus on Christ.

BECOMING PRISONERS OF THE LORD

The walls in the dream made it certain that nothing outside their perimeter could be seen. God's approach to our sanctification accomplishes the same thing. The walls of inevitable circumstance are erected for our protection and ultimately lead to an undying faith. This is because things become impossible for us to handle and we are compelled to give up looking to the outside world for hope. Instead, we choose to look exclusively to the Lord. By an act of our will, we become prisoners of God's will for our lives. Since nothing else is going to work, we decide to live in compliance with his Word. That is when we begin to experience real freedom.

In loving response to our predicament, God shows us how to walk a narrow path toward freedom in Christ. The world is meant to be harsh; its very difficulties cause us to seek our hope elsewhere. The temporal things of this life are bound to disappoint us because we are to strive for a living faith that can only be realized in the eternal Christ. For this reason, the path the old man found himself on went in only one direction—toward the tree.

The tree was the Lord, who is the Tree of Life (Rev. 22:2). He is the canopy of protection we must seek in our plight. By moving toward him, we receive a supernatural healing through the emergence of the new man we are in Christ Jesus. Paradoxically, we escape both our imprisonment to the world's trappings as well as the enemy's tactics to keep us bound to fear by choosing to be bond slaves to righteousness. Only then will we experience real freedom to be God's newest creation—men who are sold out to Jesus.

THE EMPOWERED CHRISTIAN LIFE

I pray that this book has helped to make God's Good News real to you. I also pray that in having read it, your inner man will be strengthened. Hopefully, you have been able to see what being a real man is all about. It means hearing God's Word and doing something about it. It also involves integration and application of Spirit-filled principles in your life which will empower you to cross that path in front of you. Go ahead; take the necessary steps. Faith, hope, and love are just beyond view.

The only thing holding us back is fear and the idea that being pretenders can help us cross the chasm of uncertainty below us. What a liar our carnal nature has turned out to be! The truth is that the path of faith stretching out before us is defined by our obedience to God's Word. It is a divinely appointed journey meant to show us the way to God's everlasting pleasure with us.

I will close with a prayer. May it help you express your heart's desire to be a man wholly dependent on God.

My Lord and Savior,
I pray that the Holy Spirit would fill me and that I would experience the baptism of fire from on high. Let it ignite my heart for a life that is earnest and truly dedicated to dying to the things of the flesh. I ask, Lord, that you strengthen me in order to be able to take a stand for your Word and live by its principles daily. Help me to be a hearer and doer of everything that pertains to a life of righteousness in Christ Jesus.

Forgive me of all my sins, and create in me a pure heart and sincere spirit, by which I may be certain I will live a life more pleasing to you. Father God, take my fear away and give me a spirit of boldness, so that I may be a powerful witness in this world to the truth of your love for everyone. Make me someone who can go all the way across the bridge marked "Faith and Obedience." Don't let me quit on you or give up on myself. Lastly, Lord, let your Holy Spirit teach me everything I need to know about succeeding today. Help me to stop worrying about tomorrow.

I pray that, in the end, you will be able to say to your holy angels, "Look at what my child has done. Look at the size of that temple he brought down. Isn't his faith in me something glorious?"

Thank you, Jesus, for dying for me, so that my soul might be saved in the process. Please help me bring glory to the Father. Come now, Holy Spirit, so I might have the strength to follow you all the way. In Jesus' wonderful name I pray. Amen.